Linda Barker's
HOME-MADE STYLE

Linda Barker's
HOME-MADE STYLE

100 GREAT DECORATING IDEAS

C&B

COLLINS & BROWN

Published in Great Britain in 1999 by
Collins & Brown Limited
London House, Great Eastern Wharf
Parkgate Road, London SW11 4NQ

First published in volume form by Anaya Publishers Ltd as: *Simply Fabric* (1993),
Simply Paint (1993), *Simply Colour* (1994), *Simply Paper* (1994),
Simply Curtains (1995).

British Library Cataloguing-in-Publication Data:
A catalogue record for this title is available from the British Library.

3 5 7 9 8 6 4 2

ISBN 1 85585 6913 (hardback edition)

Photographer: Lizzie Orme
Stylist: Linda Barker
Cover design: XAB Design
Cover photograph of Linda Barker: Alex MacNaughton

Printed and bound in Italy by New Interlitho

CONTENTS

INTRODUCTION

Many of us do have an irresistible urge to decorate our homes – to personalise it, mark on it our individuality, and make it home. From a new lick of paint on the woodwork to grandiose dreams and schemes, the way we adorn our homes vividly reflects our personality. An inspired choice of fabrics, papers and paints and just a little imagination can transform any drab room into a riot of fabulous effects. It needn't cost very much and it certainly doesn't require a fistful of technical qualifications, just lots of enthusiasm and a little patience. And once you've tried some of the projects in this book, that's just the beginning! From then on you can develop your own variations and adaptations – you're far more likely to run out of space before you exhaust all the colours, materials and methods at your disposal.

Colour and finish in decoration should be fun and exciting. Creating your own individual look for a room, or painting a piece of furniture, is immensely rewarding. Never be afraid to play around with different colour combinations – you can always cut out fabric swatches and lay them together before you sew, or test out your paint techniques on plywood or cardboard first.

Tool and Materials

A magpie's collection of bits and pieces is all you really need to get going, plus a place to work – there's nothing quite as infuriating as having to clear away all your carefully arranged motifs ready for découpaging just as you're getting going. A shed at the bottom of the garden would be fine if you can shut the door and be left alone to get on with it. Otherwise, a table top is perfectly acceptable so long as you can spread your materials out in front of you, and you have access to storage drawers where you can keep shells, ribbons, vibrant fabric swatches, paints, coloured papers – in fact, anything that takes your fancy.

Paint charts Invariably, we have to rely on these tiny cards when choosing wall colours. The trick is to take the paint chart into daylight with a small swatch of the fabric that may be in the room. Hold the square at arms' length and squint at it to see the effect of the colour.

Paints Use water-based paints if you can as they are kinder to the environment, simple to use and easy to wash from hands and brushes.

Specialist paints such as ceramic and glass paints are available from good art supply shops or craft outlets. Always check the labels on these products to ensure that the item to be painted can actually be used afterwards, or whether the finished objects can only be for decoration.

Gouache colour is an artist's quality paint and it can be used thinly with lots of water to create a delicate wash or thickly to create a solid area of colour, such as on the carrot image used for the kitchen wall decoration (see page 94).

Brushes For the painted projects you will need a selection of good brushes in several widths. Small brushes are suitable for craft projects, and larger brushes for some of the wall treatments – it is always good to pick up special offer multi-packs, but be aware of some of the cheaper varieties – as soon as you start to paint they may deposit stray hairs every second or third brush stroke. When you're finished, wash brushes rigorously then leave with the bristles hanging over the edge of a work top. This allows the air to flow around them so that they can dry thoroughly.

Art brushes are also available in many shapes and forms and although the initial investment may be high, these should last a long time provided you care for them.

Inexpensive paste brushes are a good investment as they save your best brushes from ending up in the glue pot.

Varnishing requires a special flat brush available from art shops and good decorating shops, and should only be used for varnishing – nothing else. Use water-based acrylic varnish whenever possible as the brushes can be quickly washed out in water.

Paint palettes and china saucers These are very convenient for mixing small quantities of paint or holding tiny amounts of glue, so it is useful to have a stack of these to hand. Use your old ones, chipped ones or the hideous pink and purple ones that were part of a bargain gift set that your elderly aunt gave you for Christmas!

Sewing machines and pins and needles
The fabric projects featured range from small hand-stitched napkin rings to more elaborate curtain treatments requiring a sewing machine of some kind, be it hand-cranked or high-tech. The majority of the projects can be completed using a straight stitch on any machine. All that is required are the common dressmaker's pins and a packet of assorted household needles.

Fabrics The project that you are working on determines the type of fabric that is needed. It is obviously sensible to use a washable fabric whenever you can, particularly for, say, a tablecloth or napkins. If more than one fabric is used for a project, and you are buying the fabrics new, study the washing labels carefully to ensure they are compatible for washing and that the colours are fast.

Fabric dyes These are sold in several forms: hot or cold water dyes, hand or machine dyes. Always try to dye fabric in a washing machine as it ensures an evenness of colour and is very convenient to use. Whichever dye you choose to work with, always read the manufacturer's instructions carefully first.

Bondaweb is a soft material that bonds fabric to fabric once it is pressed with a hot iron. This quality makes it ideal for appliqué.

Ribbons and organza are materials that, ideally, should be part of your basic work kit. These are generally bought as oddments or remnants, so if you see a pretty ribbon, buy it to add to your collection – it may turn out to be perfect for a future project. Car boot sales are excellent places for buying tied-up bundles of maybe six or seven different ribbons, of which several will be acceptable but one or even two will be particularly attractive.

Sequins, beads and buttons Buy these on a whim and store them in clean jam jars, on display if possible, to inspire new ideas. You can also raid second-hand shops and pick up clothing just for their trimmings – and this way there's a chance that you will discover some really unique finds.

Coloured papers and wrapping papers are lovely to have a supply of if you have the space to store them, and can then be purchased whenever you see one you particularly like the design of.

Filler and wallpaper paste Whether you are creating craft pieces or generally improving your home, general hardware supplies such as these are useful to have around.

Flotsam and jetsam Shells and pebbles are all beautiful things to have to hand, as is driftwood or those glorious pieces of frosted glass that start life as broken bottles and the sea turns into little jewels. You can collect feathers, bits of sheep's wool from walks in the countryside, and leaves and flowers to press – see the biscuit barrel project on page 150.

Curtain-making Techniques

There are several points to consider when creating your own curtains:

Measuring your windows Windows should be measured several times for an accurate reading, as the window will often vary slightly across the width or height because of uneven floors. Then consider the length and width of the dressing, and whether you want them to be lined or unlined.

Length Allow for turnings and hems at the top and bottom and at the sides. This can vary but recommended allowances are mentioned in each project. For curtains that drape onto the floor, add 5-10 cm (2–4 in) to the finished length for the hem, and subtract 6 mm (¼ in) from the measurement to avoid draping the fabric on the ground.

For curtains hung from a pole, measure from the base of the curtain ring. But for curtains hung from a track, make an allowance for the heading so that the track will not be exposed when the curtains are closed. Add a further few centimetres or inches for the top edge of the curtain so that it stands above the track.

For blinds, measure the finished length from the top edge of the batten or pelmet board and allow for the depth of the touch-and-close fastening if this is to be run along the top of the batten or board. The fastening can alternatively be fixed to the front edge of the batten or board and so the length is calculated from the top edge of this.

Width Curtains can extend beyond the window area, making the window seem wider than it actually is. Housing space for the curtains is often better taken up with wall space rather than window space. To establish your basic width, measure the length of the pole or track allowing for any returns, and allowing 7.5 cm/3 in for an overlap where the curtains meet at the middle.

Unlined curtains Some of the projects outlined in the book require a simple curtain construction. An unlined curtain is the simplest of all window coverings, and is ideal for the inexperienced sewer.

Measure the length of the curtain, adding 10 cm/4 in to the finished length for the hem. Also add 25 cm/10 in for a 12.5 cm/5in heading, or 15 cm/6 in for a 7.5 cm/3 in heading.

Cut the fabric drops, allowing for any pattern repeat (this will always be given on the printed edge of the fabric selvage). Join the fabric lengths using a flat seam, matching the pattern if appropriate. Turn in a double seam for the sides, pin and slipstitch or use a straight stitch on a sewing machine. Turn up the hem, once again using a double hem. Turn over the top heading and lay the heading tape along this edge. For narrow headings set the tape approximately 5 cm/2 in down from the top edge. For a wider tape, the heading should be set just 6 mm/¼ in. Pin the heading and stitch in place. Ensure that the rows of stitching start from the same edge of the curtain heading to avoid any gathering of the fabric on the right side. Trap one side of the curtain heading cords with a line of stitches and then pull the cords from the other side to gather up the heading to the required width.

Pull up the heading cords to the required finished width, loop up the excess tape and tie into a neat bundle or loop this around a purchased cord tidy. Even out the gathers at the front of the curtain using your fingers. This can be done partially when the curtains are not fixed up at the window and their final adjustment is made when the curtain is on its track and they are drawn closed.

Lined curtains Often lined curtains offer a good covering for most windows. They block more light than unlined ones, hang more substantially and offer a protection against any drafts.

Measure the length of the curtain, adding the required seam and hem allowances. The length of the main (face) fabric should have 15 cm/6 in added for the hem and 7.5 cm/3 in for the turnings at the top of the curtain. Cut the lining to the finished measurement plus 10 cm/4 in for the hem and 2.5 cm/1 in for the top turning.

The width of the curtain should be two-and-a-half times the width of the finished curtain for the correct amount of fullness. Add 7.5 cm/3 in for the side turnings of the face fabric and 5 cm/2 in for the side turnings of the lining.

Cut the fabric drops, allowing for the pattern repeat and join the pieces using a straight stitch on the sewing machine. Press the seams open. Turn over a double hem on the lining fabric and sew a line of stitches close to this fold.

Turn over 4 cm/1½ in side allowances on the face fabric and hand stitch in place, using a small herringbone stitch. Finish the two lines of side allowances stitches, 25 cm/10 in from the top and bottom of the curtain. Turn up a double 7.5 cm/3 in hem and mitre the corners. Hand stitch the hem.

Lay the lining over the face fabric so the hem of the lining lies 2.5 cm/1 in above that of the finished curtain. Turn in the edge of the lining 2.5 cm/1 in from the edge of the curtain and stitch. Fold the lining back on itself along every seam line and half width and lock the lining to the face fabric by hand sewing along this fold from top to bottom. At the other side turn the lining in as for the previous side, and stitch 2.5 cm/1 in from the edge.

Trim the top edge of both the lining fabric and the face fabric so they are aligned. Turn over 2.5cm/1 in, lay over the gathering tape, pin and stitch in position.

If you are using a narrow 2.5 cm/1 in heading tape, place it at least 5 cm/2 in down from the top edge, so that a small frill will form across the heading when the tapes are gathered. All other tapes can be stitched 12 mm/½ in from the top edge of the curtain.

Pull up the cords in the heading tape to the required width and tease the gathers with your fingers to even them out; when the curtain is hung from the track or pole the gathers may be further adjusted. Tie the cords into a neat bundle or around a cord tidy, and insert the curtain hooks into the heading tape.

LIVING ROOM PROJECTS

Of all the exciting projects in this chapter, perhaps the most effective for totally transforming the look of your living room are the soft muslin drapes on page 54. Creating an illusion of air and space, they require minimal effort on your part – they don't even need any stitching, yet the finished results are truly stunning!

Or, if you are feeling a little more ambitious, master a trick of the interior decorating trade and recreate the marbled dado panelling on page 68 to give your room a really grand feel.

Other projects such as the elegant print-room screen on page 22 and the floral firescreen on page 38 are both inspired by the seventeenth-century technique of cutting and pasting eye-catching designs. This technique can also be adapted with items such as stamps and postcards to suit smaller projects such as the letter rack on page 42. Large pieces of furniture and strong wall treatments can dominate a room so for those of you who fancy a subtle change only, try the sunburst mirror on page 52 or the cherubic papier mâché clock on page 26 to update your living room with style.

Pleated Lampshade

Good quality, attractive wrapping papers are so inexpensive you can make lampshades to complement any room in the home and change them as often as you please.

MATERIALS

lampshade frame

tape measure

wrapping paper

scissors

glue

coin

skewer

raffia

masking tape

Hints

Use a low-watt lightbulb for the lamp as anything higher may scorch the paper shade.

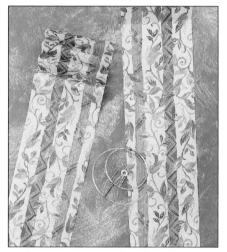

1 Measure the height of the frame and add 5cm/2in to give the depth of your shade. Measure the bottom ring of the frame and double this to give you the length of paper required. Cut out the paper, join strips with glue if necessary. Fold the paper concertina-style into 2.5cm/1in wide folds.

2 When completely folded, join the side edges together by tucking one fold inside another and securing with glue. If you have an obvious design on your paper try matching the pattern, even if you need to sacrifice the odd fold or two.

3 To cut the scalloped bottom edge, pinch together three or four folds and cut into a half circle. If you prefer, use a coin as a template while cutting. Punch holes through the centre of each fold, 2.5cm/1in from the top edge of the shade, using a skewer.

4 Thread raffia through the punched holes. Bind the ends with masking tape to make this easier. Pull the top of the shade together leaving an opening wide enough to fit over the frame. Tie the raffia. Put glue on the top and bottom rings of the frame to hold the shade in place.

Ivy Twist Tiebacks

A few strands of fake ivy add interest to this ingenious way of tying back ordinary curtains.

MATERIALS

tape measure

scissors

ivy fabric

lining fabric

thread

needle

plastic-coated garden wire

fusible webbing

iron and ironing board

fabric glue (optional)

sewing machine

brass rings

brass hooks

Hints

Use plastic-coated wire to stitch inside the tiebacks, or look for wire that will not rust in the wash.

1 Pass a cloth tape measure around your curtains at the point where the tiebacks will be to determine the length of your ivy twist. For each tieback, cut out a strip of ivy fabric and the lining fabric to this size, and hand stitch a length of wire to the reverse side of the ivy fabric, following its stem. Bend the wire into a small loop at either end to prevent the wire from sliding through the stitches.

2 Use fusible webbing and an iron to fix the lining fabric to the printed fabric, and then trim both the backing fabric and fusible webbing to match the facing fabric. If you have difficulty obtaining fusible webbing, a little fabric glue should be sufficient to bond the two fabric pieces together while you stitch around the edges.

3 Use a close zigzag stitch on your machine to stitch around the edges of the twist. Keep the fabric taut as you stitch, turning the fabric under the sewing foot as you go. For each tieback, sew a brass ring in the centre of the lining fabric and fasten it onto a hook. Finally, twist the tiebacks around the curtains.

Covered Footstool

Most footstools are covered in rather boring fabric and although I am using two colours of plain cotton, this method of cutting away one fabric to reveal another underneath is very attractive.

MATERIALS

scissors

2 pieces of contrasting fabric

chalk

pins

sewing machine

thread

staple gun

tacks

hammer

hessian

Hints

If possible, remove the legs from the footstool first as this makes fitting the fabric easier.

1 Cut the fabrics to fit over, around and just beneath the footstool. Baste the pieces together. Enlarge the template below on a photocopier to a suitable size. Use it to draw the stars on the top fabric, avoiding the fabric edges. Pin around the stars.

2 Use a contrasting thread and a close zigzag stitch on the sewing machine to stitch around the star outlines. Carefully cut inside the sewn areas on the top layer only.

3 Place the fabric right side down and lay the footstool over this. Pull the fabric over the sides and staple it to the underside of the stool, keeping the fabric taught.

4 Fold the corners to make neat mitred folds. Using tacks, attach a piece of hessian to the underside of the footstool covering the row of staples. Paint the legs to match the top and reassemble.

Star Wall Decoration

These stars can look magical in any room. Use against a mottled dark blue ceiling to create a celestial look.

MATERIALS

template paper

spray glue or sticky tape

yellow and orange stiff paper or thin cardboard

craft knife

glue

Hints

You could copy this idea in any coloured card and use for Christmas tree decorations.

1 Use a photocopier to enlarge our template to your preferred star size. For my stars the template has been enlarged by 100%, to double its size, but you could have smaller ones if you prefer. Use spray glue or tape to fix the photocopy to the cardboard and cut around this edge.

2 Fold the points of the stars following the fold lines on the template as a guide. Bend back the tabs. Glue the smaller shape to the larger one, along the tab edges. Press this into the main shape. Glue the stars to the wall along the tab edges.

Vase Decoration

This is a simple, yet decorative idea to give a unique look to an inexpensive vase or lampshade base.

MATERIALS

paper strips

paste

florist's wire

emulsion paints

household paint brush

strong adhesive

soft cloth

Hints

The paper strips are wired so they will coil easily. Experiment with longer pieces for more complicated coils.

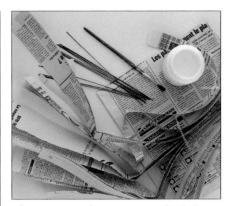

1 Moisten each paper strip with a little paste and coil this around a length of florist's wire until it is completely covered. Make sure that the ends of the wire are also covered so the wire inside is not visible.

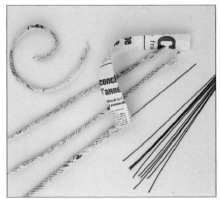

2 Use a little emulsion to paint each coil and twist it into the desired shape while the paint is still wet. Leave to dry and touch up the colour with a second coat if necessary. Use a paint colour to co-ordinate with the vase.

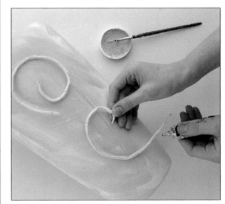

3 Stick the coils onto the vase using a strong adhesive. Leave the glue to dry and then brush a little darker shade of paint over the coils. Wipe a little off while it is still wet. You will find that some paint is held in the recesses for an unusual effect.

Print Room Screen

This type of cutting and pasting of prints was particularly popular in the seventeenth century. But the inspiration for my screen was borrowed from the many historical houses I have visited.

MATERIALS

photocopied prints	emulsion paint
photocopied borders	household brush
ruler	folding screen
set square	PVA glue diluted 50/50 with water
scissors	gloss varnish

Hints

Look for prints in second-hand shops or antique markets.
Photocopies can be tinted with tea to simulate old age.

1 Assemble the prints and borders together and use a ruler and set square to outline a variety of shapes to make a more interesting screen. It's surprising how much material you will need to cover the screen so be prepared! Cut out each design and shape ready for pasting.

2 Paint the screen with emulsion paint. Position the prints and borders on the screen. Be imaginative and don't always group the prints in a totally symmetrical way. Try framing a small print with a deep border for an original effect.

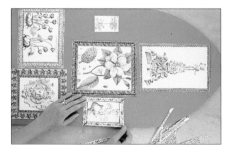

3 When you are happy with the grouping and arrangement of the prints start to glue them down. I find it easier to position and glue two sides of the border first, then glue the print in the middle, lining it up squarely to the corners. Finally glue the remaining edges of the borders.

4 If you think your screen needs more detail, look out for these wonderful printed ribbons, bows and lion heads. They are perfect for adding a theatrical touch to your screen. Cut out carefully and glue around the prints. Finish with at least two coats of gloss varnish.

Gilded
Lamp Base

Dutch Metal is considerably
cheaper than real gold leaf,
but looks almost the same,
so I think this is a wonderfully simple way to gild.
However it's a good idea to
give the lamp base a final
coat of varnish to stop it
from tarnishing.

MATERIALS

Dutch metal leaf sheets

Japan Gold Size adhesive varnish

brown coloured varnish

Hints

Any varnish is suitable, but the
brown tinted variety gives a slightly
antiqued look.

1 Gilding can be applied to any surface – ceramic, metal or plastic, although wooden lamp bases will need to be varnished first. Apply the Gold Size adhesive to the surface of the lamp base and wait until it is almost dry.

2 Take the sheets of Dutch Metal and press on to the tacky surface of the entire lamp base. Position each sheet carefully as you will not be able to remove them once they have come in contact with the Gold Size adhesive.

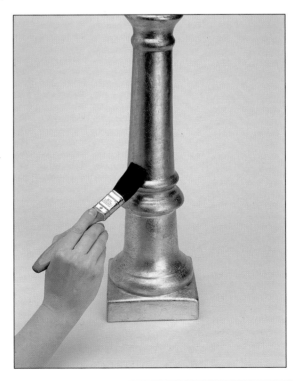

3 Rub your hand over the metal leaf to remove the loose pieces that have not adhered to the base. Make sure the surface is smooth. Paint on a layer of the coloured varnish and leave to dry.

Cherub Clock

This clock has such a stunning shape, like a grand carriage clock, that it can take pride of place on your mantelpiece.

MATERIALS

dinner plate	PVA glue diluted 50/50 with water
polyboard	craft knife
pencil/pen	wrapping paper
ruler	tea bag
wallpaper paste	skewer
music manuscript	clock mechanism
cherub patterned paper	masking tape

Hints

Polyboard is much easier to use than any of the alternatives. If it is not available, use hardboard instead.

1 Position a large dinner plate centrally on the polyboard. Mark out a border measuring 72x20.5cm/28x8in at the base of the plate. Draw around the plate and gently curve the two sides outwards to meet the edge of the border, creating a classic carriage clock shape.

2 Cut around your outline. Paste the music manuscript to the centre of the clock. Don't worry about covering the whole clock face as the cherubs will overlap and form a border. Cut the cherubs from the paper and position them around the clock. Stick down with PVA glue.

3 When the glue is dry, use a sharp craft knife to cut around the cherub details at the outer edge of the clock, keeping as much detail as you can. Cut two polyboard triangles and cover with wrapping paper for the back support.

4 Wash the surface of the clock with a cooled, wet teabag to age the appearance. Punch a hole through the centre of the clock with a skewer. Push the clock mechanism through the hole and secure at the back with a little tape. Secure the back supports in the same way.

Tied Curtain Heading

On this curtain, the gathering tape has been dyed to coordinate with the patterned fabric. This is then sewn onto the front of the curtain as part of the decorative treatment.

MATERIALS

curtain fabric

tape measure

scissors

fabric dye

heading tape

pins

ribbon

thread

sewing machine

Hints

Use a good-quality cotton heading tape for dying; synthetic materials will not take to the dye as well as natural fibres. Natural cotton ribbon may also be dyed to match rather than purchasing coloured ribbon. Follow the manufacturer's instructions when dying the tape or ribbon.

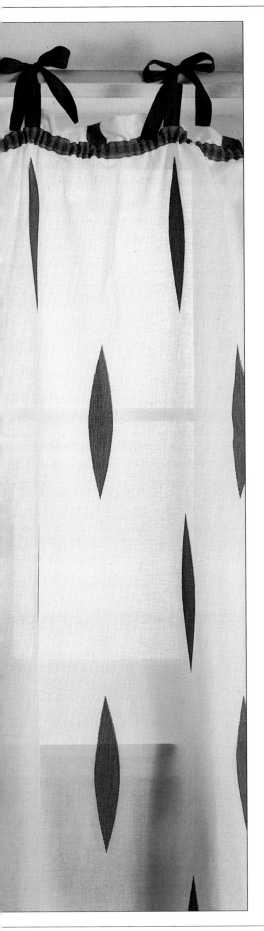

1 Measure your window carefully and follow the guidelines in the introduction for making up a simple unlined curtain. This type of heading would also suit a simple lined curtain, provided the overall effect is softly unstructured. This would be ideal for most country-style homes in living rooms and bedrooms alike.

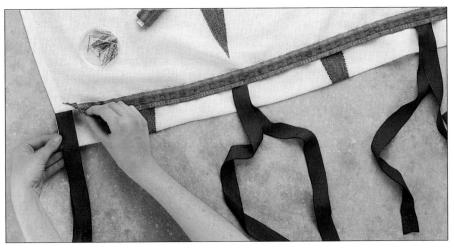

2 Pin the dyed heading tape in place leaving a gap of approximately 5cm/2in between the top of the curtain and the tape to produce a softly frilled heading that will flop over the tape. Cut 35.5cm/14in lengths of ribbon, fold in half and insert into the top of the heading at regular intervals of 25cm/10in. Stitch the heading tape in place, trapping the ribbons as you sew. Start stitching the heading tape by sewing across the heading cords at the leading edge of each curtain. Make sure the cords stay free on the outer edge. Then stitch from one end of the tape to the other, trapping the ribbons as you sew. Finally, start from the same end to stitch the lower edge of the tape. Hold the heading tape taut while you are stitching to avoid any gathering on the front of the curtain.

Fabric Padded Picture Frame

You only need a small remnant of a sumptuous raw silk to transform an old picture frame in this way.

MATERIALS

picture frame

scrap paper

pencil

scissors

silk fabric

wadding

PVA adhesive

glue brush

Hints

Choose a frame that has little or no moulding on the front as these are likely to wrinkle the fabric when it is stretched across the front of the frame.

1 Separate the glass and back from the frame. Draw around the inside and outside edges of the frame on the paper. Add 5cm/2in borders both inside and outside the frame and use this as a template to cut out a piece of fabric. Snip the inside diagonal corners of the fabric almost up to the inside frame pencil marks.

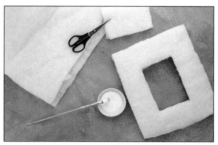

2 Cut a piece of wadding to fit over the front of the frame. Trim a sliver of wadding from the inside edge as the wadding will squash down and cover this gap when the fabric is pulled over. Glue the wadding to the frame. I used a double thickness of wadding to give a more rounded appearance.

3 Place the frame, face down, on the wrong side of the fabric, lining up the diagonal cuts on the inside and making sure the borders are even all around. Glue along the inside and outside edges of the frame. Make sure a little glue is spread to the back of the frame to hold the fabric securely. Pull the fabric over the edges and press into the glue.

4 Mitre the edges carefully to give a neat finish. If the back of the frame is visible when displayed, you may wish to cut a panel of fabric and glue this over the raw edges. Use the paper template as a pattern for the fabric. Reassemble the frame, including your chosen picture.

Marquetry Floorboards

As a border on bare wooden floors this method looks stunning and belies the true simplicity of the technique.

MATERIALS

3 colours wood varnish

stencil brushes

pre-cut stencil

masking tape

clear gloss varnish

white spirit

Hints

Check the floorboards for irregularities. Secure loose boards and sink all exposed nail heads using a hammer and nail punch. If necessary add artist's oil colours to the varnish to achieve a required shade.

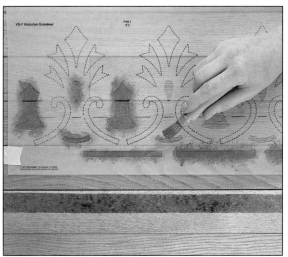

1 Create a border for the stencil design by placing two strips of masking tape on the floor about 5cm/2in apart. Infill the stripe between with the darkest shade of varnish. When dry carefully peel away the masking tape.

2 Choose a stencil that uses at least two different colours. Make sure the stencil sheets are solvent resistant. Position the first stencil sheet against the bottom edge of the varnished stripe and paint through the stencil with coloured varnish onto the floorboards.

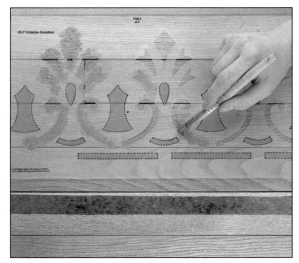

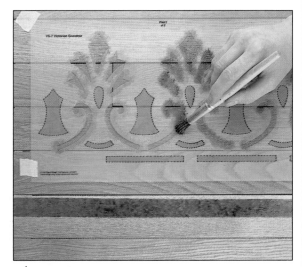

3 When the varnish is absolutely dry, position the second layer of your stencil and apply the next varnish colour. Always hold the stencil in place with masking tape and ensure that the registration lines match accurately.

4 Wait 24 hours to allow the varnishes to dry thoroughly then coat the whole design with one or two coats of hard surface varnish.

Crackle Lure
Key Cupboard

Many pieces of wooden furniture benefit from a little antiquing to give them character. Using this technique, which gives a cracked paint effect, this charming little cupboard has been transformed.

MATERIALS

white emulsion primer

white emulsion paint – base coat

coloured emulsion paint – top coat

paint brush

PVA glue

cotton wool

photocopies of statues and architecture

Crackle lure kit (containing ageing oil varnish and water based varnish)

tube of artist's oil colour (umber)

fine grade sandpaper

soft cloth

Hints

To speed the drying process once the second layer of varnish has been applied, you can blow-dry the surface with a hair-dryer.

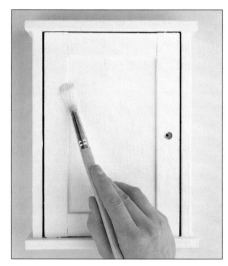

1 Prepare the cupboard by removing any existing paintwork, sanding down as necessary. Apply the white primer to the surfaces. When dry sand lightly with fine-grade sandpaper, then paint with one coat of white emulsion base coat.

2 Use a dry brush and dip the ends of the bristles into the coloured emulsion. Use a flicking motion to transfer some of the paint onto the surface. Allow to dry.

3 Use PVA to glue the photocopies within the panels of the cupboard. When dry apply the ageing varnish in a thin, even layer over the entire cupboard including the photocopies. It's a good idea to experiment first to test the drying time.

4 When the ageing varnish is almost dry, but still slightly tacky, apply a generous layer of the second, water based, varnish. Leave overnight to dry. The two types of varnish react with one another causing tiny cracks to appear in the surface of the paint.

5 To accentuate the cracks and improve the aged look, use cotton wool to rub a small amount of the umber artist's oil colour gently into the cracks. Polish off any excess with a soft cloth, taking care not to disturb or flake the cracked paint.

JOHN MAITLAND,
Duke of Lauderdale.

Marbled Column

There are many different types of marble and as a result there are probably as many techniques for marbling. I have broken down the basic principles to make a simplified version that always follows three basic steps: applying the glaze, distressing the glaze and veining.

MATERIALS

oil based paint – base coat

transparent oil glaze

tubes of artist's oil colour
(raw sienna and raw umber)

white spirit

5cm/2in paint brush

cotton cloth

fine-grade sandpaper

Fitch brush (or soft artist's brush)

artist's fine paint brush

Softening brush
(or long-haired paint brush)

paint kettle

Hints

It's useful to have a piece of marble to refer to when creating this effect so why not do as I did and treat yourself to a marble pastry board – or simply borrow a reference book from the library.

1 Prepare the plastic column for painting by 'keying' the surface with fine sandpaper. Apply two coats of oil based base coat. Mix a little raw sienna colour with about one tablespoon each of white spirit and oil glaze in a paint kettle and paint thinly over the column.

2 Wrap the cotton cloth into a small pad and wipe away varying sized 'pebble' shapes from the wet glaze. To get a real marble effect, rub off long thin shapes surrounded by clusters of smaller round shapes.

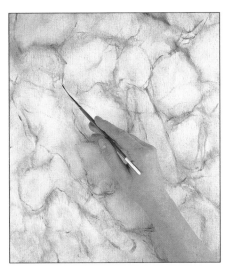

3 Use a long-haired artist's brush and lightly flick it across the whole surface. This will blur and soften the marks you have created without obliterating the colour and will still retain the overall marble effect.

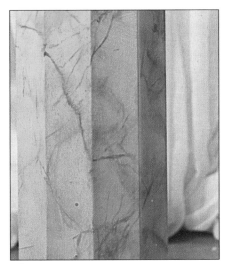

4 Thin the raw umber colour with a little white spirit and paint on the 'veins' with an artist's brush. Paint in one direction, but occasionally, cross these lines diagonally with more 'veins'. When dry, use a high gloss varnish to seal and protect the marbling.

Floral
Firescreen

If you don't have a fireplace you could make a feature of this screen simply by placing it in a corner of the room.

MATERIALS

hardboard base

fretsaw

scissors

floral wrapping paper

pencil

household paint brush

emulsion paint

PVA glue

strong adhesive

varnish

Hints

Place a sheet of wrapping paper on the hardboard. Use its height and width as a guide around which to draw an elongated circle. This may be wider than the paper at some points. Draw a wavy line through this and cut out with a fretsaw.

1 Cut out lots of individual flower and fruit motifs from the wrapping paper. If the flowers are printed against a dark background, don't worry too much about trimming right up to the edges. Keep one sheet whole for the background.

2 Paint the back of the screen and a narrow border around the front with emulsion paint. Glue the whole sheet of paper to the front of the screen, trimming around the fruit and flowers motifs at the top edge so they fit into the curves. Stick on individually cut flowers to fill the gaps.

3 Use tiny flowers and butterflies cut from the rest of the wrapping paper to add interest. Make a stand for the screen by cutting two 90 degree triangles from the excess hardboard. Coat with emulsion paint. Glue to the back of the screen with strong adhesive. Protect the front of the screen with three coats of varnish.

Stencilled Floor Cloth

Floor cloths are as old as time but they never seem to go out of fashion. Remember when the cloth has been sealed, it is extremely hard wearing.

MATERIALS

canvas – floor cloth weight

pre-cut stencil

emulsion paints for stencilling

stencil brush

PVA glue

paint brush

polyurethane varnish

scissors

masking tape

Hints

Roll and press the stencil brush firmly into the canvas as you are painting to make sure that the emulsion paint penetrates the weave.

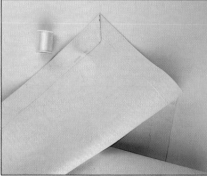

1 Cut the canvas according to the size of floor cloth you want. This canvas is available in very large widths so you could get two small cloths from one width. Turn under the raw edges of the canvas and stitch on a machine or glue turnings in place.

2 Position the stencil to form a border on the cloth. Hold in place with masking tape. To produce depth and subtlety in my design, I used three paint colours. Before each shade was dry, I carefully blended the next shade on top while allowing the first to show through.

3 Use the same technique to stencil in the central design. Before doing so it's advisable to determine the middle of your cloth. The simplest way to do this is to fold it into quarters, pressing firmly along the creases to pinpoint the exact centre.

4 When the emulsion is quite dry, paint on a layer of PVA glue. Leave this to dry. Repeat the process until you have built up four layers of adhesive. When the last coat is dry, protect the cloth with a final layer of polyurethane varnish.

Letter Rack

If you keep losing bills and forgetting to write letters, this decorative rack is the ideal organiser.

MATERIALS

cardboard	paper for layering
pencil	wallpaper paste
dinner plate	wrapping paper
tea plate	heart motif
saucer	string
scissors	sealing wax
ruler	coin
gummed paper strip	plasticine

Hints

I used a wrapping paper printed with stamps and postmarks but if you can't find anything similar use a collage of old letters and real stamps instead.

1 On a piece of cardboard draw the outlines of a dinner plate, tea plate and saucer. Cut around the curved edges and across the centre and sides for each section. You will see that each diminishes in size. Cut a cardboard base to the length of the dinner plate's diameter and 12.5cm/5in wide.

2 Use gummed paper strips to assemble the letter rack as shown. Paste torn paper pieces over the entire cardboard surface. Build up at least five layers. Alternate the direction of each layer and allow each to dry before applying the next.

3 Tear the printed wrapping paper into varying sized pieces and, using the wallpaper paste to apply, cover the letter rack. Build up an interesting collage effect. Some pieces may also be cut as a contrast to the torn edges.

4 For the final decorative touch glue cut-out hearts at random over the surface, then bind the rack with string for a packaged look. Apply sealing wax to the string joins then stick a coin into the plasticine and use to press firmly into the soft wax leaving a distinctive impression.

Picture Frame

If you want to surround simple photographs or pictures, this is an attractive idea for a unique and inexpensive frame.

MATERIALS

craft knife

cardboard

bradawl or skewer

scissors

paste

handmade paper

brush

paper fasteners

coiled paper ribbon

masking tape

Hints

To use as a picture frame for a wall, simply extend the paper ribbon between two top corners to form a hanging loop.

1 Cut four cardboard frame pieces each 5x30cm/2x12in. Place together in a square formation so that each corner overlaps the next creating a cross shape. Using the bradawl punch a hole through the centre of each of the four corner joins.

2 Again using the bradawl, punch a pattern of holes down each side of the frame keeping the holes at least 1cm/3/8in apart. Cut and paste handmade paper over the front of the frame pieces, making sure that the paper overlaps to the back.

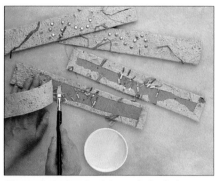

3 Push the bradawl through the holes in the cardboard to pierce the handmade paper covering each piece. Insert a paper fastener into each hole (apart from those at the corners) for decoration. Flatten the fastener tabs at the back. Neaten the back of the frame with a strip of handmade paper.

4 Assemble the four sides together as shown, aligning the four holes at the corners. Re-emphasise these four holes with another twist of the bradawl. Thread with a piece of coiled ribbon, knotting at the front and back. Leave approx 5cm/2in at the front before cutting. Fan out the ribbon.

5 Cut a square of cardboard to cover the back of the frame and secure with masking tape. To make a stand for the frame, simply cut out a cardboard support for the back and attach it to the frame with tape. Cover with handmade paper if you wish.

Dado Border

This is an inexpensive way of creating a unique look for any room. I have used a sophisticated border for a living room, but you could copy a child's drawing to create a personal border for a bedroom.

MATERIALS

tape measure

image to be copied

sponge

water

gummed paper strip

wooden board

sepia watercolour paint

artist's paint brush

craft knife

wallpaper paste

Hints

If you prefer, use the border at picture rail height or to define a small window or doorway.

1 Measure the width of the walls where you want to use the border. Measure the length of your chosen image, then divide this figure into the width of your walls to give you the number of photocopies needed. Copy enough border pieces plus four or five extra.

2 To prevent the paper strips from wrinkling when pasted to the wall, pre-stretch them by applying a wet sponge to the front and back of each piece. Use the gummed paper strip to stick each to a wooden board. Don't worry if a little black dye comes out of the prints.

3 While the border strips are still damp, tint the surface with diluted watercolour. Leave the strips to dry overnight. Use a craft knife to remove them from the board, making sure the edges are quite square. Use wallpaper paste to position on your wall approx. 81.5cm/32in from the floor.

Dress Curtain & Tails

This dress curtain is designed to loop over a pole in a series of swags and fall at one side with a decorative finish.

MATERIALS

pattern paper

fabric - top

fabric - lining

scissors

pins

string

pencil

needle

thread

Hints

The easiest way to estimate the length of the swagged curtain is to wind a length of string around your pole creating the swags and tails you want to achieve in fabric.

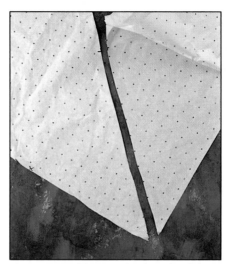

1 Cut your fabric to the length of the string adding 1.25cm/½in all round for turnings. Cut a 90cm/36in square from pattern paper for the tail template. Mark a point 30cm/12in up from the bottom left corner. Mark another point 30cm/12in to the right of this. Draw a line to join the points. Cut out.

2 Position the template on the front of the fabric, on the left hand corner of the narrowest edge. Pin then cut the fabric along the diagonal line, extending it as far as you need to cut the corner off the fabric. Cut a piece of lining fabric to the same shape.

3 Pin, then sew the two pieces of fabric together using the seam allowances. Leave a gap to turn the fabric to the right side, then stitch closed. Press the seams flat. Drape over the pole, pleating the tail into neat folds.

Tassels

Use these tassels to tie back your curtains or to decorate cushions or pelmets.

MATERIALS

wooden beads – 3 sizes

glue

card

scissors

crochet thread

needle

Hints

For decorative effects you can use different shades of crochet thread to match all the colours in your room.

1 Glue the beads with the smallest at the top. Measure then double the height, add 5cm/2in. Cut a piece of card to this length and 10cm/4in wide. Wind crochet thread round the card 50 times. Remove from card. Use end thread to wind around threads to form a tassel.

2 Place these tassel threads over the beads and spread out evenly to surround beads. Gather the threads below the bottom bead and again bind with more thread and knot securely.

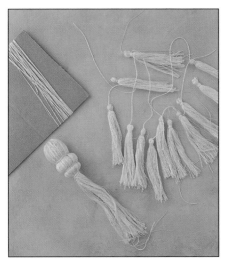

3 Wind more thread around the two points where the beads join, to create the top of the tassel. Use the same piece of card to create at least twelve more tassels as before. These should all be the same thickness but could be in different colours.

4 Sew these tassels around the bottom edge of the largest bead in the tassel top, spacing them evenly to give a full effect. Attach a triple loop of threads to the top of the beaded tassel, winding more thread around the base of the loop to secure.

Sunburst Mirror

Truly fanciful, this mirror will add a decorative touch to any wall. The shape also makes an imaginative picture frame.

MATERIALS

pencil

corrugated cardboard

paper pulp

gesso powder

bowl

household paint brush

sandpaper

metallic paint

gloss varnish

strong adhesive

small mirror

plate hooks

Hints

Use plate hooks attached to the back of the mirror to hang it on the wall.

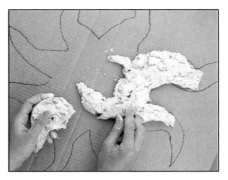

1 Decide on the overall size of the mirror. Draw a circle to this dimension on the corrugated cardboard, with a smaller circle, at least 15cm/6in diameter, in the centre. Outline the eight points of your sun burst shape between the two circles. Apply the paper pulp within the shape leaving central circle uncovered.

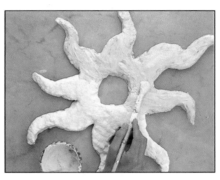

2 Remove the paper pulp shape from the cardboard when dry. Mix the gesso powder in a bowl and paint two layers over the front and back surfaces of the sun shape. Allow the first coat to dry before applying the second and sand down between coats for a smoother finish.

3 Paint the sun shape with a water-based metallic paint. The surface will be slightly uneven, so push the paint into the small lumps and bumps until it is completely covered. Protect the finished mirror frame with two layers of gloss varnish. Use a strong adhesive to stick the mirror to the back of the frame.

Decorative Bowl

I love the bizarre shape of this bowl, which will make an eye-catching centrepiece for any table.

MATERIALS

tin snips	paper pulp
chicken wire	emulsion paint
protective gloves	household paint brush
pliers	gilt wax
florist's wire	matt varnish

Hints

Chicken wire can be quite difficult to mould so always wear protective gloves.

1 Cut chicken wire into a 35.5x51cm/
14x20in rectangle and two
5x30cm/2x12in pieces. Wearing gloves and
using pliers, twist the rectangle into a tube
shape. Squeeze wire together about
20cm/8in from one end, then sculpt the
bowl and stand. Create the decorative
shapes from the narrow wire pieces.

2 Cut 15cm/6in lengths of florist's wire
and use to join the decorative pieces to
the bowl. Push one end of the wire through
the decorative piece, then through the bowl.
Twist to hold together, then snip off excess
wire with pliers. Repeat at each end.

3 Apply the paper pulp to the bowl in
small amounts until it is completely
covered both inside and out. Stand the bowl
upright and smooth out the pulp to a
thickness of 1.2cm/1/2in. Roll a small ball of
pulp and position on top of one twisted side
decoration.

4 When the pulp is dry, apply coloured
emulsion paint to the inside and outside
of the bowl and one side decoration. Use
the gilt wax to colour the remaining side
decoration. Apply with your fingers, rubbing
well into the textured surface. Finish with a
coat of matt varnish.

Muslin Drapes

These are created without any stitching using three layers of muslin which are tacked or stapled to the top of the wooden architrave that surrounds the window.

MATERIALS

tape measure

muslin

scissors

staple gun/tacks

Hints

If you don't like the idea of white muslin, why not dye it first to a shade that will complement your colour scheme?

1 Measure the window and cut enough muslin to cover it completely. Tack or staple the required number of drops to cover the window, overlapping if necessary but without any fullness or gathering. Use double thickness for privacy.

2 Cut two lengths of muslin three times the depth of the window. Using double thickness of muslin, tack or staple one narrow edge straight onto the window frame on the right. Repeat with the other narrow edge on the left hand side. The muslin will now fall in a huge loop.

3 Gather the loop together in the middle and tie into a huge, soft knot to hang in the centre of the window. This can be tricky but easily achieved with an assistant. Spread the bottom edge to drape evenly along the floor. Cut a length of muslin to the width of the window. Staple or tack along the top of the architrave to disguise the other layers. Gather intermittently from the bottom edge to form loops and tack in place on the architrave. This gives a softly swagged finish.

Ribbonwork Cushion

The simplicity of this cushion cover reminds me of the weaving I used to do as a child and yet the design looks quite sophisticated.

MATERIALS

4 patterned or plain ribbons

cotton fabric

pins

scissors

thread

cushion pad

Hints

Make your cushion cover a little smaller than the pad to give your cushion a plump look.

Preparation

Choose patterned and plain ribbons of varying widths for the best results. Contrasting colours are strong visually so I have used orange and red with green, but lilac and yellow would be equally vibrant. Cut the cotton fabric to the same size as your pad.

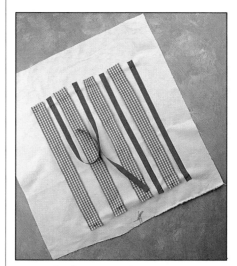

1 Pin the first two ribbons onto the cotton backing keeping an even spacing between the edges. If you pin at right angles to the ribbon edge you will be able to sew over the pins without having to remove them first.

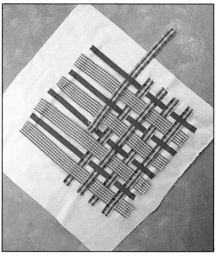

2 Take the third ribbon and weave this between the first two ribbons. Weave over the first ribbon then under the second ribbon. The next weave will then start by going under the first then over the second. Continue until the third colour is finished.

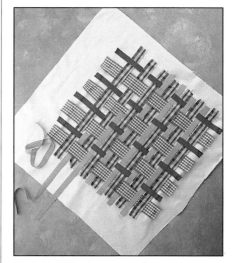

3 Follow the last procedure to weave the fourth ribbon, until all the gaps have been filled with ribbons. Remember to pin each ribbon at right angles every time you complete a row.

4 Cut two more pieces of cotton to the pad size. Place one square over the worked ribbons. Fold back a third then pin and sew to the cushion top around the three sides. Repeat with the second square to form an envelope opening. Turn through to the right side.

Star Motif Bowl

This attractive bowl is ideal for displaying pot pourri, fruit or dried flower heads.

MATERIALS

shallow bowl

cling film

paper pulp

large spoon

gesso powder

small dish

household paint brush

scissors

gold paper

emulsion paint

Hints

A shallow bowl is the easiest shape on which to mould paper pulp. When you become more experienced, experiment with a variety of different shapes.

1 Line the inside of your bowl with cling film. This acts as a releasing agent enabling you to remove the dried pulp easily. Coat the inside of the bowl with pulp using the back of a spoon to press it evenly into the curves. Maintain a thickness of 1.2cm/1/2in. Remove when dry. Press a thin sausage shaped piece of pulp to the base to form a support, leave to dry.

2 Mix the gesso powder in a dish, according to the manufacturer's instructions. Paint over the inside and outside surfaces of the bowl. The gesso will even out lumps and bumps creating a smoother finish. Additional coats of gesso will result in a more professional finish.

3 Cut the gold paper into star shapes and apply to the bowl while the gesso is still wet. You will find that they will stick quite easily to the surface. Don't worry if some gesso seeps over the stars, I think this adds character. Paint with emulsion.

Beaded Holdbacks

These jewelled holdbacks look good around a pair of curtains at a conventional dado height.

MATERIALS

self-cover holdback

fabric pieces

translucent fabric

scissors

pencil

beads

thread

needle

Hints

To make a guide for stitching on the tiny beads, place a self-cover holdback on each circle of fabric and draw a pencil line lightly around its circumference. Sew on the beads within this line.

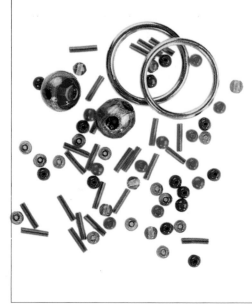

1 For each holdback, cut a fabric circle using the self-cover holdback as a guide, remembering to leave sufficient allowance for drawing-up the fabric beneath the button. Cut a layer of translucent fabric and place this over the base fabric for a pretty effect. Sew the beads onto the face fabric until the base is almost covered. Make a line of running stitches around the outside of the circle.

2 Pull up the running stitches and slip the cover over the holdback. Pull the stitching thread further to fold all the raw edges over to the back of the holdback. Press on the second half of the holdback, snapping the two pieces firmly together. Screw the fixings to the base of the holdbacks and fix into your wall.

1 Pass a cloth tape measure around your curtain at the point where the tieback will be to determine its length and transfer this measurement onto a piece of paper. Draw a 15cm/6in line at the centre of this line at right angles and 7.5cm/3in lines at either end. Connect the points to make your pelmet template. For each tieback, cut a piece from the face fabric and stitch beads onto it following my example above.

2 Again using the paper template as a guide, cut a piece from the lining fabric. With right sides facing, stitch the face fabric to the lining with a seam allowance of 12mm/½in. Leave a small gap, turn the right sides out and neatly hand stitch the gap closed.

3 Sew a small brass ring to each end of the tiebacks and use them to secure the tiebacks to the wall-mounted hooks. Pull the curtains back to the sides of the window, wrap the tiebacks around them and pass the rings over the hooks. To close the curtains, release one ring of the tiebacks and allow them to drop down.

Beaded Tiebacks

Transform plain tiebacks with a few tiny beads. These simple flower decorations look best when stitched against an unpatterned fabric.

MATERIALS

tape measure

paper

pencil

ruler

scissors

fabric for tieback

beads

thread

needle

lining for tieback

sewing machine (optional)

brass rings

brass hooks

Hints

Look for small packets of mixed beads in craft shops and department stores. A few beads go a long way.

Colour-washed Blinds

Colour-washed blinds are replacing plain ones in many of the design and decorating shops, so here's a quick way of creating that up-to-the-minute look without spending a fortune.

MATERIALS

oil-based paint

turpentine

paint bucket

wooden Venetian-type blind

soft cloth

paintbrush

Hints

Open the blind to its maximum drop to paint it, and place it on several layers of newspaper to protect your work surface. Paint one side of the blind first and leave it to dry before turning the blind over to work on the other side.

1 Mix four parts of paint to one part of turpentine in the paint bucket. For my blind I wanted quite an opaque paint, allowing only a hint of the wood colour to show through. If your blind is quite battered, this is probably your best option, but if you want a lighter look, simply add more turpentine.

2 Spread the blind in front of you so that the slats do not touch each other. Dip the soft cloth into the prepared paint. Rub the paint onto the surface of each slat as if you were cleaning it. Do not worry if the paint seeps into the cords as these look better colour-matched.

3 Use the same technique to paint the top covering strip (if your blind has one), and colour match any other parts of the blind such as the acorn cord holder on this one. On these small pieces, you may find it easier to brush on the paint and then wipe off the excess with a cloth. Use a very thin version of the paint to colour-match all the cords.

Gilded Shell Pole

Use either the flat part or the curved top of these pretty shells.

MATERIALS

dowelling	wood glue
saw	PVA adhesive
shells	Dutch metal leaf (or gold paint)
yellow emulsion paint	acrylic varnish
paintbrush	pole rings
drawer handles	bonding glue

Hints

If it is difficult to obtain small quantities of Dutch metal leaf, use gold paint. But make sure it is good quality - you can usually tell by the price, and cheaper paints are often rather dull.

1 Cut a length of dowelling to the size of the required pole; remember to exclude the finial ends. Paint this and the shells with a coat of pale yellow emulsion paint. You will also need to paint two small drawer handles to attach to the ends of the pole.

2 Use strong wood glue to secure the drawer handles to the ends of the dowelling pole. Hold the two pieces together for a little while to make sure they are firmly stuck together. Release and allow to dry completely.

3 Brush a thin layer of PVA adhesive over the pole (but not the drawer handles) and the front of the shells. When it is almost dry - the glue should be tacky - press the metal leaf over the surface and it should adhere easily. Remove the backing paper and rub away the excess foil. Paint on a coat of acrylic varnish and leave to dry.

4 If you are using rings, slide them onto the pole and then use a strong bonding glue to attach the shells onto the ends. If the shells are flat, bonding is slightly easier. Curved shells may need propping forward with a piece of cork or wood so that they lie straight.

Stencilled Lampshade

I have used a sharp blade to cut along a few of the stencilled outlines, which gives this pretty lampshade a delicate three-dimensional pattern and allows the light to pass through.

MATERIALS

thick cartridge paper

craft knife

pre-cut stencil

acrylic stencil paints

stencil brush

saucer

adhesive

Hints

If you don't have a stencil brush use any small square ended brush or trim the bristles of an ordinary paint brush.

1 Plain lampshades are perfect to stencil but if you want to reproduce an existing shade simply remove it from its frame and draw around it on a piece of cartridge paper. Cut out the flat shape, allowing 2.5cm/1in extra all round for turnings.

2 Position your stencil on the shade with spray adhesive. Pour a little stencil paint into a saucer and apply the paint sparingly with light circular strokes to the shade. Remember if you are stencilling a fabric-coated shade, use fabric stencil paints.

3 When the paint is dry, use a craft knife to cut along some of the stencilled outlines and ease away from the shade so a little lamp light shines through. Snip the turning allocation of a new lamp shade, fold these edges under the frame and glue with strong adhesive.

Marbled Dado Panelling

This marbling technique uses quick-drying emulsion paints. I have made the panelling from pieces of wallpaper, which means you can work on a flat surface, then simply cut and paste the marbled panel to the wall when finished.

MATERIALS

white emulsion paint – base coat	artist's fine paint brush
vinyl wallpaper	feather
2 colours emulsion paint – top coats	paint kettle
emulsion glaze	high gloss varnish
tube of artist's acrylic paint	saucer
cotton cloth	pencil
5cm/2in, and 10cm/4in paint brushes	scissors
long-haired paint brush for softening	

Hints

Give an attractive finish to your paper panels by cutting them to fit under the dado rail, then using a saucer as a guide, mark and cut out inwardly curving corners. Paste to a plain painted wall with ordinary wallpaper paste.

1 Apply white emulsion base coat to a piece of wallpaper. Mix equal amounts of the coloured emulsion with the glaze. Paint the glaze mix on to the wallpaper surface using a wide brush. While the glaze is still wet progress to the next step.

2 Twist a cotton cloth into a sausage shape, place on to the glazed surface and simply roll off the glaze as if you were rolling pastry. Shake out and retwist the cloth occasionally. Follow the same direction all the time until you have ragged the whole surface.

3 Add a little artist's acrylic paint to darken the top colour and mix with a little glaze and water. Paint sparingly in a diagonal direction from left to right, then right to left across the paper. Soften the edges by brushing lightly with a dry long-haired brush.

Plaster-effect Walls

This is one of my favourite techniques and is called plaster effect because when the three colours are combined they give a lovely soft appearance of new plasterwork.

MATERIALS

white emulsion paint – base coat

light, medium and dark emulsion paint – top coats

emulsion glaze

cellulose decorator's sponge

paint tray

paint kettles

1 Paint the walls using two base coats of white emulsion. Mix together each of the three coloured top coats with equal quantities of glaze and water. Blend each mixture well in separate paint kettles.

2 Pour a little of the darkest paint/glaze mix into a paint tray. Dip the sponge lightly into this and apply it to the surface using a circular 'scrubbing' action to create a cloudy layer of colour. This takes practice but the effect is better than using a paint brush.

3 When the surface is dry, apply the second, medium-coloured glaze. This should be used sparingly to maintain a cloudy layer while allowing the underlying colour to show through in patches. If the second colour is too dense, rub off with a clean cloth.

4 When dry apply the lightest paint/glaze mix. Again this is applied very sparingly and is intended simply to soften the whole effect while giving just a hint of colour. If at this stage you feel the overall effect is too light, reapply the first colour.

4 Using a fine artist's brush dipped in the white base colour, paint diagonal 'veins' across the surface of the softened bands of colour. While these 'veins' are still wet, lightly stroke with a feather to soften their outline. When dry, finish with a high gloss varnish.

Splattered Picture Frame

This method of splatter painting is sometimes known as Cissing. For this picture frame I have splattered over a silver base coat as this gives a wonderfully luminous quality to the finished frame.

MATERIALS

shellac varnish

artist's silver powder

2 tubes of artist's oil colours

white spirit

paint brush

polyurethane varnish

paint kettle

sandpaper

ruler

Hints

If you don't intend to use this paint finish often, shellac varnish may be an expensive buy, so use a solvent-based, silver paint for the base coat instead.

1 Prepare the frame by sanding down the wood to a smooth finish if necessary. Mix a little of the silver powder with the shellac varnish to form a thin base coat. When you apply this to the frame it will produce an interesting opaque finish. Allow to dry.

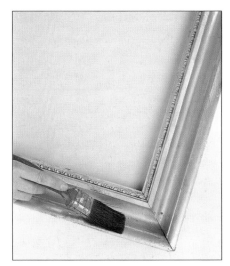

2 Paint one coat of polyurethane varnish over the silver top coat. This is an unusual, though essential, application as it forms the basis for the overall splattered effect. Do not let it dry out completely before progressing to the next step.

3 Thin the 2 oil colours individually with a little white spirit and dab each colour on to the frame so they sit on top of the varnish. Don't worry if the colours touch and start to run together – that's exactly what they should do!

4 Dip the tip of the paint brush into white spirit and splatter the solvent on to the frame by striking the brush against a ruler. The painted surface will now open up, forming unusual pools of colour. Leave to dry horizontally.

Display Shelves

Hung with little raffia tassels, these neat display shelves look attractive and provide useful storage for a kitchen or bathroom.

Hints

Decorate the shelving with beads or feathers as an alternative to the raffia.

1 Decide on the length and width of the shelving. Cut a piece of cardboard to this size plus an extra 7.5cm/3in all round for the depth of the shelves. With a closed pair of scissors score the cardboard 7.5cm\3in in from each edge. Cut out squares at each corner. Fold up the sides and tape together with gummed paper strip.

2 Cut strips of cardboard 7.5cm/3in wide for the shelves. Use a ruler to mark their positions, keeping them an even distance apart and varying their lengths and arrangement for a more interesting look. Fix the shelves in place using the gummed strip along all edges for added support.

3 Measure the spaces between the shelves and cut strips of handmade paper to fit these areas. Use paste to stick in position. This distinctive paper with its fern leaf detail is perfect for the shelving.

4 Cover the outside of the unit with corrugated paper starting with the shortest sides. Cut the paper a little longer than these sides to wrap around the corners. Make 7.5cm/3in cuts in the paper at the points where the shelves meet the sides so you can tuck the paper inside easily.

5 Line the internal shelves with brown paper covering above and below each shelf. Cut the paper to the exact size as there should be no overlap along these edges. Where one shelf meets another, snip the paper and smooth neatly into the corners. Paste down.

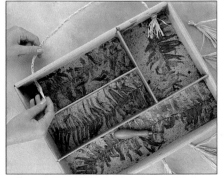

6 Make two holes in the top of the unit using the bradawl. Thread a length of plaited raffia through the holes, wrapping the ends with tape to make threading easier. Knot and fray the ends.

KITCHEN & DINING ROOM PROJECTS

These two rooms are devoted to the fine arts of eating and drinking, so it is fitting that the projects in this chapter should include a traditional patchwork tablecloth on page 132, painted wine glasses on page 89, brightly coloured ceramics on page 76 and place mats on page 134, all of which will add a riot of colour and texture to your kitchen and dining room. Decorating your kitchen with photocopied prints of fruit and vegetables as shown on page 94 is a cheap and easy way of bringing a touch of colour to your walls – use magazines, catalogues or your favourite books for inspiration. Creating a pretty Delft tile look from your own lino-cut stencil couldn't be easier (see page 106) and transforming a country kitchen table with a simple potato print top, as shown on page 112, is simple yet incredibly effective.

Painted Ceramics

These thermo-hardening ceramic colours (see page 118) can be purchased in lots of different hues so you can easily transform your plain china with bright patterns, just as I did here.

MATERIALS

chinagraph marker pencil

plain white ceramics

ruler (optional)

thermohardening ceramic paints

paintbrushes

palette

Hints

Let each colour dry thoroughly before painting on the next one otherwise the colours tend to merge together and become dirty.

1 Use a chinagraph marker to mark on a noughts and crosses-type grid across the flat surface of the china. You could use a ruler to determine the distance between the lines but I favour slight fluctuations in the size of each square to give a more handcrafted quality.

2 Paint the first square using a little ceramic paint. Paint the edges of the square first, then fill it in. Don't worry about letting the brush marks show in the paint - I feel that this is all part of the charm. Continue painting with this colour, building up a pattern as I have done.

3 Apply the second colour in the same way. Continue around the jug as I have done, slowly building up the checked pattern. Try to keep the colours quite thin as the top colour will overlap these and will not dry successfully if the paint is too thick.

4 Use a fine brush and a steady hand to paint in the thin lines that form the tartan finish. Occasionally the paint may blob or you may run out of paint,but don't worry about this. Allow the paint to dry thoroughly before baking the china in the oven according to the instructions on the paint.

Gerbera Bowl

This wonderful decoration for a simple papier-mâché bowl was achieved by pressing two gerbera flower heads under a colour photocopier.

MATERIALS

beach ball

newspaper

lining paper

wallpaper paste

scissors

cardboard

white emulsion paint

2 vibrant colours of emulsion paint

gerberas

paper glue

paintbrush

acrylic varnish

Hints

Build up alternate layers of newspaper and lining paper dipped in wallpaper paste over half a beach ball. Allow each layer to dry before applying the next. Once the bowl has about three layers it can be removed from the ball. Use scissors to trim a neat edge around the bowl, making subsequent layers easier to apply. Five layers should be sufficient.

1 Finish the final layer with lining paper and place three wide discs of cardboard underneath the bowl to make a base. Cover the base in the same way, until it is covered and feels quite secure. Allow to dry overnight.

2 Paint the inside and outside of the bowl with two coats of white emulsion paint letting each coat dry before applying the next one. Paint one vibrant shade on the inside and the other on the outside of the bowl. I used acid green on the inside so that my photocopied gerberas would show clearly, and bright orange on the outside of the bowl.

3 Put the gerbera heads directly on the glass of a colour photocopier and make eight copies. Cut around each printed flower carefully and glue to the inside edge of the bowl. When dry, protect with two layers of acrylic varnish.

Two-toned Napkins

Use this panelling technique to make a small square of fabric into a large napkin: the more expensive the fabric, the deeper the border should be.

MATERIALS

plain fabric
patterned fabric
iron and ironing board
bias binding
sewing machine
threads (2 colours)

Hints

Choose fabrics that can be washed together and avoid those that are for dry cleaning only.

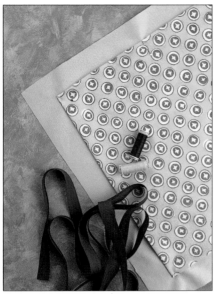

1 Cut the plain fabric to the required size of your napkin (40cm/16in is a generous size), but it could be larger or smaller as you wish. Trim your patterned fabric into a smaller square and turn under the raw edges with a hot iron. Choose a coloured bias binding to complement the fabrics.

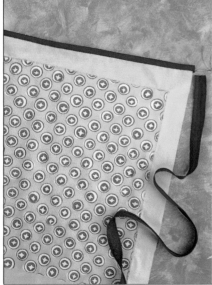

2 Pin the patterned square on to the plain fabric ensuring the borders are even all round. Use a close zigzag machine stitch to sew in place. Stitch the raw edge of the binding to the wrong side of the napkin, turn over to trap the raw edge and sew closed. Use four separate binding pieces for the neatest edging.

Vegetable Napkin Rings

Choose a decorative border with more than one element to its design for this decorative effect.

MATERIALS

ruler	green paper
pencil	printed paper border
corrugated cardboard	green card
scissors	craft knife
gummed paper strip	strong glue
paper for layering	spray-on varnish
wallpaper paste	

Hints

Use a bottle to support the napkin ring while coating the outside with varnish. When dry varnish the inside of the ring.

1 Using a ruler and pencil, draw two 18x5cm/7x2in rectangles on corrugated cardboard. Cut out each rectangle and twist into a ring. Secure the join with a gummed paper strip. Tear the paper into strips ready for layering.

2 Apply paper strips to each ring with wallpaper paste. Alternate the direction of each layer until you have built up five layers. Allow to dry between each layer. Glue small strips of green paper to the inside of each napkin ring to line. Don't worry if the dye seeps through.

3 Choose a paper border with a definite design like mine. I cut the checked edge from my paper border and used wallpaper paste to stick it in bands around the outside of each napkin ring. The vegetable prints were then glued to a piece of green card before cutting out with a craft knife.

4 Use strong glue to stick the vegetable prints securely to the front of each napkin ring. Wait until this is completely dry before coating inside and out with a layer of varnish. The varnish will also considerably strengthen the ring.

Spice Rack

Distressed colour allows one colour to show through another and often works best when two contrasting colours are used together, as on this spice rack.

MATERIALS

plain spice rack

pink emulsion paint

blue emulsion paint

small paintbrushes

sandpaper (medium grade)

Hints

On larger objects you will find it easier to remove the top layer of emulsion paint from its base coat if you rub some hard wax between the layers.

1 Using pink emulsion and a small paintbrush to reach the corners, paint a base coat on to the spice rack. When this is dry, cover with a layer of the blue top coat. You needn't worry about applying this coat with the same careful coverage as for the first colour since most of it will be removed.

2 When the blue emulsion layer is quite dry, start to wear away the top surface with the sandpaper. It will be more interesting if you rub certain areas more than others and in some places the natural wood could even show through.

Tea Towel Blind

Coloured tea towels make brilliant coverings for windows. Stitch together as many as it takes to cover the window.

MATERIALS

wooden batten (5 x 2.5cm/2 x 1in)

touch-and-close fastener

fabric glue

screw eyes

tape measure

tea towels

thread

scissors

casing fabric

dowelling rods

saw

curtain rings

blind cord

brass rings

acorn

cleat

Hints

To hang the blind at a window, screw a wooden batten onto the frame. Glue one side of a strip of touch-and-close fastener to this. Fix screw eyes to the bottom edge of the batten to correspond with the rings on the blind.

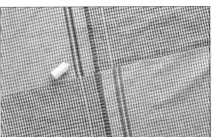

1 Measure the width and drop required to cover the window and stitch the towels together to match these measurements. If you need to piece the towels, sew a double hem at the raw edges to prevent fraying.

2 In contrasting fabric, cut strips that are 9cm/3 ½in deep and the same width as the blind plus 2.5cm/1in for the end hems. These will be the casings for the dowelling rods and the size of the window will determine how many you will need. Leave about 30cm/12in between each casing. Lay the blind flat and leaving a distance of approximately 5cm/2in from the bottom and 23cm/9in from the top, measure the position of the casings. Pin and then stitch the casings to the blind keeping the seams horizontal. Saw the dowelling to the right length and slide into the casings.

3 Sew the other half of the touch-and-close fastener to the top of the blind. Then sew the curtain rings to the bottom edge of each casing at intervals of 50cm/20in and 5cm/2in in from each edge. Thread the cord through the rings (including the batten), taking the cords to one side of the blind. Attach the blind to the batten and finally attach an acorn and cleat to hold the cords.

Mosaic Wine Coasters

At last I have found a use for all those brightly coloured odd tiles I collected from car boot sales, but since most tile suppliers are happy to sell odd tiles, you can soon build up an eclectic assortment.

MATERIALS

paper

pencil

hardboard

fret saw

sandpaper (fine grade)

tile adhesive/grout

spreader

coloured tiles

hammer

cotton cloth

felt

PVA adhesive

glue brush

Hints

Place each tile between several thicknesses of newspaper and give it a few sharp taps with a hammer to break it into tiny mosaic pieces.

1 Enlarge the template from this page on a photocopier to a suitable size. Alternatively, draw your own pattern on paper using the base of a wine glass as a size guide. Cut this shape from the paper and use it as a template to draw on the hardboard.

2 Cut around each shape carefully using a fret saw and use a small piece of fine-grade sandpaper to smooth any uneven edges. Use the spreader to skim a thin layer of tile adhesive/grout over the top surface of the coaster, trying to maintain an even thickness.

3 Break the tiles into small pieces (see Hints, left) and build up a pattern on the coaster starting in the centre and working outwards. On some coasters I have followed the shape of the coaster when making the pattern and on others I have started with a daisy shape and filled the mosaic pieces around this.

4 Leave the mosaic to set, then apply a thick layer of tile adhesive/grout over the whole coaster, pushing it between the mosaic pieces and around the edges of the coaster. Scrape off the excess grout and wipe the surface clear with a damp cloth before the adhesive/grout dries. Cut a felt backing and glue it to the bottom.

Painted Wine Glasses

These ordinary wine glasses are given a colourful treatment using glass paints which dry to a water-resistant finish. Although they are reasonably hard wearing don't attempt to put them in the dishwasher.

MATERIALS

glasses

tube of black glass relief paint

glass paints

fine paintbrushes

palette for mixing paint

scissors

Hints

Most glass paints are transparent. But if you prefer the opaque qualities I have used here, simply mix a little white glass paint with the transparent colour.

1 Place the glass to be decorated over one of the motifs on this page (enlarge the motif on a photocopier if necessary), close one eye and outline the image using the black relief paint directly on to the glass. It only works with one eye closed! Try to squeeze the tube evenly so the outline is consistent - you may want to practise on paper first.

2 Paint the glass in as many colours as you like. I used three separate colours for this glass, but you could easily use more colours or just one if you prefer. I would prefer several glasses, each painted in a different way, but it's up to you. Allow each colour to dry before using the next.

3 Paint inside the relief area using a contrasting colour so that the design has more impact (all glass colours can be mixed to produce different colours if required). Leave to dry overnight so they become rock hard.

4 When the glass is quite dry, etch into the painted glass with a closed pair of scissors. I have etched small scrolls into the glass rim and a zigzag pattern around the base, but vary your patterns on each glass. The glasses should only be washed by hand.

Country-style Egg Cupboard

The quality of this coloured photocopy is so good you would have to look twice to realize that it's not a high quality print. It's such a very clever way of turning a simple little cupboard into something out of the ordinary.

MATERIALS

glass-fronted cupboard	tin snips
chicken photograph	brown gummed tape
scissors	panel pins (optional)
hardboard	hammer (optional)
saw	oil-based paint or emulsion paint
chicken wire	paintbrush

Hints

Any simple glass-fronted cupboard can be given this treatment. The wooden shelves inside have been drilled at regular intervals using a 7.5cm/3in drill bit which provide just the right support for the eggs. It could also be used to display a collection of decorative eggs.

1 Select your favourite photograph of a chicken. If, like my photograph, the top of the print is dark, cut it away and replace with the lighter parts from another photograph to make a montage. Place it on a colour photocopier and enlarge it so that you have a print to fit the cupboard panel.

2 Cut the hardboard to the same size as the glass panel and glue the print on to the front. Snip out a piece of chicken wire using the hardboard as a template and lay it inside the glass door.

3 Place the hardboard over the chicken wire, ensuring the chicken is the right way up. Secure the panel to the door using gummed tape, and panel pins if necessary. If you need to use panel pins be careful not to break the glass: lay the cupboard on a padded surface and tap the pins in at an angle.

4 If, like this one, the cupboard has been varnished you will need to paint the frame using oil-based paint. If not, you will be able to use emulsion or water-based paints. Put in the wooden shelves and hang the cupboard securely on the wall.

Colourful Roller Blind

Most plain bamboo roller blinds can be given this colourful treatment - match the colour to your walls.

MATERIALS

roller blind

emulsion paint

plastic container

paintbrush

fabric

scissors

PVA adhesive

glue brush

needle

thread

Hints

Stretch the blind gently as you paint it to open up the weave so these gaps don't become clogged with paint.

1 Mix together a solution of paint and water using equal quantities of each in the plastic container. Unroll the blind on to sheets of newspaper and pull back the cord to protect it from the splashy paint. Paint the front, leave to dry, and then turn over to paint the back.

2 Cut two strips of fabric to the length of the blind and one strip to the width of the blind. Each strip should be 7.5cm/3in wide. Stitch a small seam down the edges of each strip. Spread glue along the inside of the longer strips, fold in half and cover each edge of the blind with one strip.

3 Spread glue along the inside edge of the smaller strip and fold the ends inwards to make an arrow-shaped point. Fold in half and slip the blind inside the fabric strip as before. The arrow head mitres the fabric, making a neater finish.

4 Use an invisible stitch to secure the fabric binding to the blind. Push the needle through all the thicknesses, pull the thread tight and then pull the needle through to the front again. Continue along all three sides. Reassemble the cords and hang the blind according to the instructions.

Kitchen Wall Treatment

Colour each photocopy individually or use a colour photocopier, either way your kitchen walls will be far from boring.

MATERIALS

black-and-white photocopies

scissors

gouache colours

wallpaper paste

paintbrush

Hints

If you can find a vegetable print in a gardening magazine or catalogue, use this if you prefer.

1 Photocopy six individual motifs from the original on this page, enlarging if necessary. Then assemble these and place onto the photocopier so that the next copy has six motifs printed on it. Colour the motifs simply using two gouache colours, then copy this on a colour photocopier until you have enough motifs to cover the walls.

2 Cut each motif from the copy paper and paste these on to the wall using wallpaper paste. Arrange the motifs around the kitchen fittings as you wish: it is better if they don't form a regular pattern.

Punched Tin Hearts Storage Box

Coloured tin shapes are simple to make from aluminium cans and
look so attractive that I guarantee you'll be looking for other surfaces
to decorate in this way.

MATERIALS

aluminium can	hammer
all-purpose scissors	enamel paint
marker pen	paintbrush
piece of wood	flat headed tacks
nail	

Hints

The aluminium may be cut with an old pair of scissors, but don't be tempted to use
your best pair unless you want them to be blunted.

1 Trace the outlines from this page
enlarging on a photographer if
necessary. Cut the top and bottom from
the aluminium can and, using the heart
template, transfer the outline to the wrong
side of the can with the marker pen. Cut
out the tin hearts. Protect your hands with
gloves at this stage as the tin can be sharp.

2 Place the tin hearts on the wood and
punch a series of tiny holes around the
edge of the hearts using the nail and
hammer. For a pretty effect, keep the holes
as close together as possible. I also punched
a tiny heart shape inside the larger heart.

3 Decorate some or all of the hearts with a
little enamel paint and allow to dry.
Then secure each heart to the box using
small, flat-headed tacks - I used five tacks
around each heart. If the ends of the tacks
come through to the other side of the box
you will need to file them down.

Verdigris Table Decorations

Verdigris occurs as a natural oxidization process on brass or copper: this reaction can be speeded up with the use of special chemicals, available from good craft shops.

MATERIALS

brass- or copperware

sandpaper

verdigris chemical

saucer

plastic gloves

small, stiff-bristled paintbrush

Hints

Once brass or copper has been given a verdigris treatment, it should only be used for decorative purposes.

1 Rub the surfaces to be treated with sandpaper until they become covered with tiny scratches and all the shininess has disappeared. Smaller pieces such as curtain rings can be prepared with emery paper and steel wool.

2 Pour a little of the chemical solution into a saucer and protect your hands with plastic gloves. Dip the paintbrush into the solution and work it into the pitted brass surface. After a few minutes you will start to see a greeny tinge appearing.

3 After the first coat has dried, apply a second layer of the chemical - this should greatly improve the colour of the verdigris. If necessary, continue applying coats of the solution until the desired patina is achieved.

String Vase

This wonderful vase started life as two plain plastic containers. I stuck them together and decorated them with a gooey mixture of paint and filler with the odd length of string thrown in.

MATERIALS

2 plastic containers

strong adhesive (epoxy resin)

filler

blue emulsion paint

old paintbrush

Hints

I think this spiral design looks good wrapped around the vase but you could shape the string into any number of different formations, or experiment with bands that are closer together or further apart.

1 Use a strong glue to secure the bases of the containers together and give them a good tug once they are dry to make sure they are going to stay stuck. Mix the filler with enough emulsion paint to give you a thick paste; you may need to add a little water as emulsion paints and fillers vary in consistency.

2 Cover the first 25cm/10in of string with some of the paste - be prepared to get completely messy at this stage. Lay the end of the string along the edge of one container and begin to bind it around the containers, painting on more paste as needed.

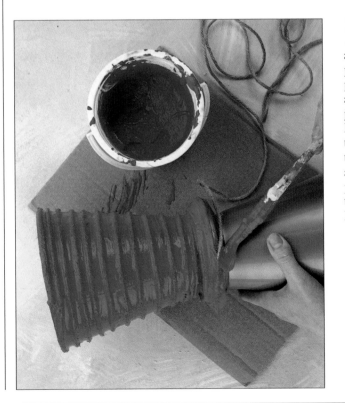

3 Continue spiralling the string around and take care to progress as neatly as possible over the point at which the containers join. The paste takes a little time to harden so there is time to remove the string and start again if necessary. Paint paste 2.5cm/1in inside the top rim and then leave to dry.

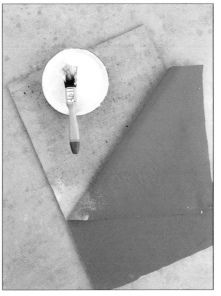

1 Carefully remove the frame from the notice board by stripping off the back tape or removing the fastenings. If these can be re-used, keep them on one side and use again when reassembling. Strip the old material covering from the board and glue down a piece of felt cut to the same size, using PVA adhesive.

2 Position the first piece of ribbon diagonally across the board and secure the ends with tacks. Use a ruler to position three parallel rows of ribbon on each side of this first one, keeping the distance between ribbons equal. Secure as before, then repeat across the other diagonal to form a diamond pattern.

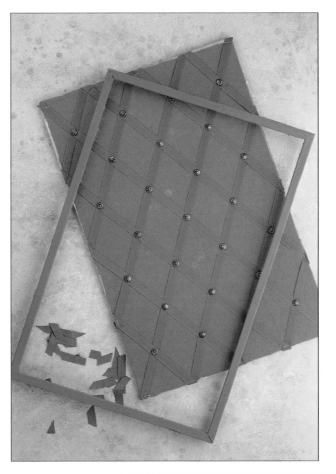

3 Push tacks through the ribbons at the points where the ribbons cross. Remove the tacks from the outer edge and staple or glue these outer ribbons down. Use emulsion to paint the frame and wait for it to dry before reassembling. Secure the board to the frame using tape or panel pins.

Ragged Chair

You'll enjoy the almost instantaneous finish you get with this technique which I find just as easy to master as sponging.
With very little effort you can achieve really professional results.

MATERIALS

coloured oil based paint – base coat

white oil based paint – top coat

transparent oil glaze

paint brush

cotton rag

white spirit

sandpaper

paint kettle

Hints

Other materials can be used to remove the glaze, such as plastic or paper bags, lightweight muslin or heavyweight hessian. Each material will give a slightly different effect.

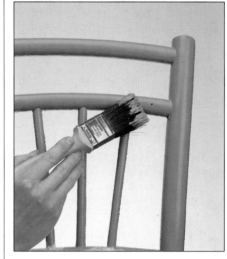

1 Prepare the chair by removing any old paint, then sanding the surface to a smooth finish. Paint with two coats of your chosen base colour. Allow to dry thoroughly and sand down with a fine grade sandpaper between each coat.

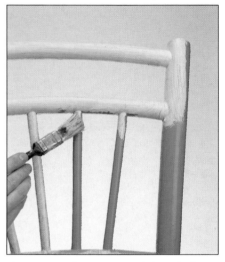

2 Mix equal quantities of the oil glaze with the white oil based top coat in a paint kettle. Paint the surface of the chair with a thin layer of this glaze mix. Be careful not to allow the paint to build up in the corners.

3 Loosely crumple the rag and press into the wet glaze. As you lift off the cloth you remove some of the glaze. Repeat with swift movements all over the chair. When the cloth is covered with glaze, shake it out and recrumple before continuing to complete the ragging.

Felt Notice Board

It seems to me that it is impossible to buy anything vaguely connected to the office in anything other than black, white or shades of grey. But most homes these days have a notice board of some description - even if it's only to pin the shopping list to - so customize your own with brightly coloured felt.

MATERIALS

notice board

coloured felt

scissors

PVA adhesive

glue brush

ribbon

ruler

decorative headed tacks

stapler (optional)

emulsion paint

paintbrush

masking tape or panel pins

Hints

Use a contrasting ribbon for the most dramatic effect or criss-cross lots of different coloured ribbons.

Lino Printed Wall

I love 'cheating' designs and this is one of the best ways to produce a Delft tile look for a kitchen or bathroom wall without the expense of buying the real thing!

MATERIALS

15cm/6in square of lino

lino cutting tool or heavy duty craft knife

coloured emulsion paint

artist's acrylic paint

pre-cut stencil

artist's brush

felt tipped pen

newspaper

Hints

Delft tiles can be bought from tiling specialists and feature many pretty designs. You could consider buying just one tile to use as inspiration for your own stencil.

1 Draw a simple pattern in each corner of the lino square with a felt tipped pen. Carefully cut around the design with a lino cutting tool. Remove the excess lino so that the pattern stands proud ready for printing.

2 Using an artist's brush apply the emulsion paint to the patterned areas on the lino tile. Press the tile onto newspaper until the pattern shows clearly, then begin patterning your chosen area of wall. The pattern should produce a square tile effect.

3 Use a fine artist's brush to paint the coloured emulsion paint onto the wall. This should simulate the fine grout lines that exist between real tiles. These lines can be painted in sketchily to enhance the design.

4 Take a small pre-cut stencil design – I chose a little chicken – and use to stencil, here and there, in the middle of your previously stencilled tile area. Use the same coloured emulsion paint, but lowlight with a darker shade of artist's acrylic paint.

Studded Glass Bowl

The glass beads on this glass bowl are normally used for flower arrangements but I couldn't resist decorating the sides of this bowl with them.

MATERIALS

glass bowl

chinagraph marker pencil

tape measure

self-adhesive plastic

top from glass paint bottle

scissors

glass paint

saucer

stencil brush

glass beads

glass bond glue

Hints

Wait for a sunny day to glue the glass beads to the bowl as the bonding solution needs ultraviolet light to work.

1 Using the chinagraph pencil, mark eight points around the top of the bowl: use the tape measure across the centre of the bowl as a guide. Cut eight small discs from the self-adhesive plastic using the top of the glass paint bottle as a template.

2 Peel the backing paper from the plastic discs and position them over the chinagraph marks. Pour a little glass paint into a saucer and dip the ends of the stencil brush in. Paint the outside of the bowl using a stippling motion, spiralling the paint as you work.

3 When the glass paint has dried to the touch, peel off the discs of plastic. The glass paint needs 24 hours to be really dry enough to use and this often depends on how dry or damp the atmosphere is. If in doubt, leave the bowl for several days before use.

4 Glue the beads to the glass - you can do this when the paint is touch dry. Using the glass bond, glue one bead in each circle of clear glass. Adhere the beads near a window to allow the ultraviolet light to set the glue. You can wipe the bowl clean after use but do not put it in a dishwasher.

Decorative Painted Candlestick

So often you can find inexpensive plain, black metal ornaments which with a simple paint treatment can be totally transformed into something much more colourful and interesting.

MATERIALS

coloured emulsion paint

white emulsion paint

gloss paint

paint brush

artist's paint brush

paint kettle

1 My candlestick was embellished with a twirling leaf design, so it was a natural inclination to highlight these areas with leaf green emulsion paint.

2 Mix equal quantities of white emulsion paint with water in a paint kettle. Apply lightly to the painted areas to give a soft, powdery appearance to suggest age.

3 Paint in other details like flowers with gloss paint to create contrast and an interesting high shine detail.

Freehand Painted Server Cabinet

If you don't have any confidence with freehand artwork, just try this stylised New England tree design. It really is so simple if you follow my steps.

MATERIALS

oil based primer

2 colours oil based paint – top coat

artist's oil colours

artist's brush

white spirit

sandpaper

antiquing wax

cotton cloth

Hints

Any cupboard door with a central panel or even a panelled internal door can be painted in this way.

Prepare the cabinet by first sanding down, then apply the oil based primer. Using the darkest oil based top coat, paint the cupboard surround. The door panels should be painted with the lighter oil based top coat.

1 I have broken down the elements for the simple tree. First paint the tree trunk and branches using the artist's oil colour and brush. Use long sweeping strokes for the branches.

2 Add the simple leaf shapes to the branches by pressing the bristles of the brush firmly against the surface and removing carefully. The leaves don't need to touch the branches.

3 Paint in the simplified bird using three shapes to suggest its head, body and tail. Add the small detail of the plant at the base of the tree in the same way as you painted to the leaves.

4 Apply a little of the antiquing wax to a soft cloth and rub gently all over the surface of the cupboard. This will give an attractive aged look to the surface of the furniture.

Vegetable Printed Kitchen Table

Who would believe that the humble potato print we all experimented with at school could produce such an ingenious pattern for a table top? I think it gives the table a pretty, French provincial look.

MATERIALS

white acrylic primer

white emulsion paint – base coat

coloured emulsion paint – printing

potato

knife

sandpaper

felt tipped pen

pencil

ruler

saucer

newspaper

Hints

As you work with the potato it can become very slippery, so you could make a handle for it by sticking a fork into its back. Alternatively wear rubber gloves to get a better grip.

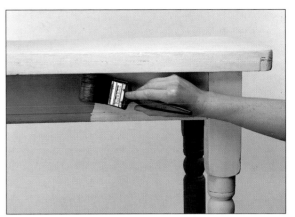

1 Prepare the table by first sanding down then priming the top. Paint the legs with basecoat only. Don't worry if the table top is uneven as this will add to its country look. Use the pencil and ruler to divide the top into 15cm/6in squares.

2 Cut a large potato in half and draw your design onto the surface with a felt tipped pen. Cut around the pattern shapes in the potato and remove the excess pieces so the pattern stands proud. I cut two shapes, one to outline the tile, shown here, the other to print the design.

3 Pour a little of the emulsion paint into a saucer and dip the potato into the paint. Test the pattern on a sheet of newspaper before printing. I printed the tile outline over the pencil drawn lines first, then applied the second design to the centre.

Woodgrained Cupboard

I make no attempt to reproduce an authentic woodgrained finish here – this technique is purely for fun! I think it's quite striking and you'll be surprised how fantastically simple it is to achieve.

MATERIALS

coloured emulsion paint – base coat

white emulsion paint – top coat

emulsion glaze

5cm/2in paint brush

rubber wood graining tool

fine grade sandpaper

paint kettle

Hints

If the woodgrain isn't quite right the first time, just brush over the still wet glaze and have another attempt.

1 Prepare the cupboard for wood-graining by removing old paint, sanding down as necessary. Apply two coats of the base coat paint. Allow to dry thoroughly and lightly sand down between each application.

2 Mix equal quantities of the white emulsion with the glaze in a paint kettle. Blend well. Paint over the central panels of the cupboard as this is the only area to be woodgrained. The remainder of the cupboard is left plain

3 Pull the rubber wood graining tool through the wet glaze. Start at the top of the panel and work slowly downwards. Rock the tool gently once or twice as you progress to achieve the dramatic woodgrain effect.

Limewashed Old-fashioned Food Cupboard

This is a simple technique that simulates an age-old finish. It is easy to achieve and cheaper than most techniques as it uses only a small quantity of white emulsion.

MATERIALS

white emulsion paint

5cm/2in paint brush

paint kettle

cotton cloth

masking tape

medium/coarse grade wire wool

sanding block

medium/fine sandpaper

Hints

New wood is not very porous, so you may find it useful to prepare it with a medium/coarse grade wire wool which will 'key' the surface, enabling it to hold the paint better. Always work in the direction of the wood grain.

1 The surface of the wood needs to be absolutely clean and free from dirt and grease. I used a sanding block to prepare the storage box before painting. Start with a medium grade sandpaper and finish with a fine grade for a really smooth surface.

2 Apply masking tape to those areas not to be painted. This not only protects the unpainted surface but gives a neat finish to your storage box as well. Remember to peel away carefully.

3 Dilute emulsion paint with water in a paint kettle. The amount varies according to the porosity of the wood, so test a small area first, making sure the wood grain is clearly visible. Apply the thinned emulsion a little at a time in small workable sections.

4 Use a cotton cloth to rub the still-wet emulsion into the wood. The desired effect is for the emulsion to leave a faint veil of white over the surface, with a thicker white appearance where the emulsion has held in the grain of the wood.

Sponged Ceramics

Use commercially prepared ceramic colours which are "thermo-hardening", meaning they should be baked in the oven. This gives the colours a very hard and scratch-resistant surface, although the ceramics should not be washed in the dishwasher.

MATERIALS

small sea sponge

ceramic colours

scissors

pencil

brown paper

small plate

double-sided tape or spray adhesive

saucer

pre-cut stencil

masking tape

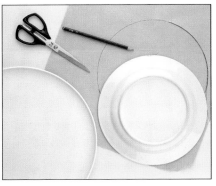

1 Clean the surface of the ceramics with soapy water to remove any dirt or grease. Before decorating a plate, prepare a mask from brown paper. Place a smaller plate, the same diameter as the centre of your plate, on the paper, draw around, then cut out.

2 Secure the mask to the plate with double-sided tape or spray adhesive. Pour a little ceramic paint into a saucer and lightly press the sponge into the paint. Dab the sponge over the unmasked area of the plate, turning it each time to create an irregular pattern.

3 Apply subsequent colours with a clean, dry sponge. When the border is dry, position the first stencil layer on the plate. Secure with masking tape. Again pour the first ceramic colour to be used into a saucer and follow the same sponging technique.

4 Allow the ceramic paint to dry thoroughly before positioning any subsequent layers of the stencil and repeating the stencilling. If you want a denser colour on some areas of the pattern, use the sponge to build up further layers of colour.

5 Again let the colour dry before positioning the last stencil layer and applying the remaining colour as before. When this paint is dry, put the plate in the oven. Follow the paint manufacturers' directions and bake for the required period of time.

Tea Tray

Images of tea cups, pots and jugs were the perfect decoration for this tray. Remember if you are photocopying from a source book be sure to use one that has a free copyright.

MATERIALS

photocopied designs

scissors

tray

craft knife

watercolours

artist's paint brush

spray paint

sandpaper

PVA glue

gloss varnish

Hints

If you can't be bothered to paint lots of little images, choose just one large central motif.

1 Photocopying can be expensive so select a page from a copyright-free booklet with the most illustrations to choose from. Randomly cut out a variety of the images until you have enough to cover your tray completely in a pleasing design.

2 Carefully cut around each image again, this time using a craft knife to get as close to the printed edge as you can. Use watercolours to paint each image. The black and white gradations on the photocopy will help you to define and highlight the shading in the right areas.

3 I used a pale pink spray paint to colour my tray. When this was dry I carefully rubbed off some pink paint with sandpaper. This revealed a little of the original green colour beneath to simulate aging. Glue the images to the tray. When dry protect the surface with three layers of varnish.

Spice Storage Boxes

These unique little containers soon replaced the conventional glass storage jars in my kitchen.

MATERIALS

watercolours

artist's brush

small wooden boxes

sandpaper

photocopied pictures

pinking scissors

PVA glue

crepe paper

darning needle

string

brass eyelets

raffia

paper ribbon

Hints

I colour-photocopied small herb pictures from a gardening book to decorate the front of these boxes.

1 Using the watercolours, paint a thin layer of colour over all four sides of the boxes. When dry, lightly rub the surface with sandpaper to remove some of the printed lettering and a little watercolour paint. This creates a pleasant, weathered finish to the box.

2 Choose a picture to represent the contents of each storage box and make a colour photocopy. Use the reducing and enlarging facility on the machine to achieve the right image size for your box. Cut the edges with pinking scissors and glue onto the front of the box.

3 Make a bag from crepe paper. The base should be slightly larger than the box base. The width of each side is equal to two sides of the box and the height is two and a half times that of the box. Thread a darning needle with fine string and sew the bag together. Cut the top with pinking scissors.

4 Position the eyelets approx 10cm/4in from the top edge of the crepe paper bag and thread through with raffia. Tie a 5cm/2in piece of paper ribbon to each end of the raffia and tease open to create a pretty fan. Put a bag inside each storage box.

Star Candlestick

Some wrapping papers are just too good to throw away after use, so I have chosen one of my favourites to decorate this candlestick.

MATERIALS

corrugated cardboard

pencil

ruler

scissors

craft knife

masking tape

paper for layering

wallpaper paste

wrapping paper

gloss varnish

Hints

If you find it impossible to draw a star freehand, use a star-shaped biscuit cutter for your outline.

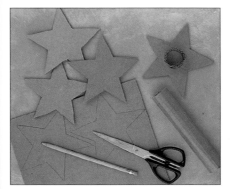

1 Draw a five-pointed star within a 10cm/4in diameter circle on the cardboard. Cut out three star shapes. Cut a 2.5cm/1in diameter circle in the centre of one star. Make a tube from an 18x7.5cm/7x3in piece of cardboard. Cut 2.5cm/1in from one end and push into the centre of the cut star.

2 Use masking tape to secure and cover the base of this star - this is the candlestick top. Join the remaining stars to one end of the tube with masking tape. Glue the candlestick top to the other end of the tube. Coat with five layers of paper using the wallpaper paste. Allow to dry thoroughly between layers.

3 Use patterned wrapping paper to decorate the candlestick. Tear some paper pieces and cut others for a more interesting appearance. Apply to the candlestick with wallpaper paste. Allow to dry thoroughly then protect with a coat of varnish.

Cafe Mug Rack

Mug racks are so useful but are often very plain so I decided to make a feature of this one and pattern it with a photocopied sign.

MATERIALS

piece of wood	wire wool
photocopied image	sandpaper
PVA glue	watercolours
household paint brush	artist's paint brush
emulsion paint (terracotta and white)	brass hooks

Hints

Find a cafe or menu sign which would look fun in a kitchen and enlarge the image on a photocopier to fit the wooden rack.

1 Select a piece of wood for your rack measuring approx. 38x15cm/15x6in and at least 2.5cm/1in thick to hold the hooks. Use these dimensions to make the photocopy enlargement. Glue the photocopy to the wood with PVA glue.

2 Use a dry brush to paint an uneven layer of terracotta emulsion paint over the front surface of the wood. Allow the black and white image of the photocopy to show through. When dry remove a little paint by rubbing the surface carefully with wire wool and sandpaper.

3 Use black watercolour to paint over some of the lettering to give it an individual hand-painted quality. Use other colours to paint in further details shown on your image. I used green paint to define the leaf pattern on my design.

4 Use the white emulsion paint to highlight some of the lettering and contrast with the previously applied black paint. Dilute the paint with 50% water and paint broad, mottled patches over the sign to give it an aged and faded appearance. Mount the brass hooks.

Découpaged Kitchen Table

This decoration is a delightful way to pattern an old or scratched table.

MATERIALS

fruit wrapping paper

scissors

PVA glue

chalk string

household brush

emulsion paint

varnish

Hints

If you are decorating an unpainted table prepare the area to take the découpage by rubbing the surface with a fine-grade sandpaper to roughen the surface.

1 Cut out the fruit images from the wrapping papers. You may have to cut images from a few papers to give you enough fruits to go all the way around the edge of the table. Remember to include any leaves that may be a part of the design.

2 Use the PVA to stick the fruits around the edge of the table to form a deep border. Ensure that you paste right up to the edges of each fruit and leaves. For a smooth finish press the fruits onto the table being careful not to overlap the paper.

3 To accentuate the découpage edge I have painted a dilute layer of emulsion over the border. If you don't have a steady hand mark out the border with white chalk. To do this tie chalk to a length of string measuring the diameter of the table, less the width of the border. Hold the free end under the thumb in the table centre and pulling the string taut mark out the circle in chalk. Dilute the paint 50/50 with water and use a wide brush to quickly cover the area. While the paint is still wet remove the paint from the surface of the découpage and some from between the fruits for an attractive edge. Varnish to seal surface.

Kitchen Cupboard Door Trellis

If you'd like a new look for your kitchen cupboards, simply transform your existing doors with this painted paper trellis.

MATERIALS

cartridge paper

pencil

craft knife

ruler

wallpaper

green emulsion paint

set square

household paint brush

PVA glue

photocopied flowers

varnish

Hints

If you have melamine doors paint them with eggshell paint, together with the relevant primer and undercoat. Wooden doors will need stripping with a hard surface remover before painting with emulsion paint.

1 Make a template for the trellis from cartridge paper cut to the size of the door panel. If there isn't a panel, make a paper one 5cm/2in narrower all round than the door. Cut wallpaper to cover each door panel and paint with green emulsion.

2 On the cartridge paper template draw a border line 2.5cm/1in from each side. Using the set square and starting in one corner at the border line draw diagonal lines across the panel, 2.5cm/1in apart. Repeat from the opposite corner to complete the trellis design.

3 Place cartridge paper panel over wallpaper panel. Cut out the squares between the trellis lines, through both panels. Allow 3mm/1/8in on each side of the drawn line before cutting. You now have a cartridge paper template and a wallpaper panel for the first door.

4 Place the flowers under a colour photocopier. I used a tiny flower to fit easily inside the small trellis diamonds. Cut out photocopied flowers and glue one flower inside a trellis diamond to form a regular pattern across the door. Varnish.

Kitchen Wall Decoration

I love the originality of using photocopies as a wall decoration in this kitchen and you won't believe how simple it is to create!

MATERIALS

rustic animal prints

craft knife

A4 bond paper

household paint brush

wallpaper paste

PVA glue diluted 50/50 with water

cotton cloth

watercolours

paint brushes

Hints

This photocopied image can be used effectively as a border or frieze as well as an all-over pattern.

1 Select the images to be used. I have chosen rustic prints from one of the many copyright-free books. Cut out and paste each image to be used onto a sheet of plain paper. Photocopy this page to give you enough prints to cover your walls.

2 Cut out each print carefully, as close to the outline as you can. Use a paint brush and the diluted PVA glue to coat both sides of each print, then stick onto the wall. Smooth flat with a cotton cloth to remove any trapped air and excess glue.

3 If your kitchen walls are not white, the photocopied print may stand out too much, so colourwash the prints with a diluted solution of the kitchen wall paint until the outline blends in well. Use the watercolours to tint each print. Protect with the diluted PVA.

Patchwork Tablecloth

Although not strictly patchwork this tablecloth makes use of two fabrics that are sewn together to make a striking cover for this kitchen table.

MATERIALS

tape measure

fabric – main

fabric – border

scissors

pattern paper

dustbin lid

tassels

needle

thread

pins

Hints

When you have cut all the pattern pieces use a close zigzag to finish all the raw edges to stop the fabric from fraying.

1 Measure the length and width of the table. Cut a piece of fabric to this size and add 1.25cm/½in for the seam allowance. Using a contrasting fabric cut out four border strips, 10cm/4in wide and long enough to edge the cloth. Cut a paper template for the curved sections using a clean dustbin lid to give you a large curve.

2 Right sides facing pin then sew the border strips to the main fabric. Allow a good overlap at each corner. Sew right into the corner point. Diagonally fold back the strips. Sew along this diagonal line, where the strips meet, to form a mitred corner.

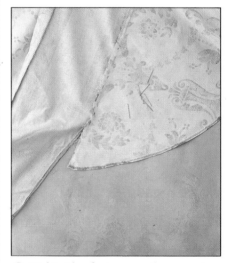

3 Right sides facing sew the curved fabric section to the border fabric. The curves should be placed so they do not quite meet the mitred corners. Turn in and sew around the hem of the curves.

4 Sew a ready-made tassel to each of the four points. Press the cloth with an iron and place it on the table at an angle with the tassels at the centre of the four sides, to show off the softly rounded edges.

Pretty Place Mats

I like this quick and simple technique and have made several sets of mats for different occasions.

MATERIALS

fabric

matching thread

scissors

dinner plate

Hints

You don't need to make all your mats in the same colour. Sometimes they can look more interesting in mismatched colours.

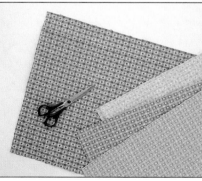

1 Choose a loosely woven fabric that will fray easily. Use a large dinner plate to determine the basic size of your mat then cut a rectangular shape, in the fabric, at least 10cm/4in larger all round the plate, so that it will fit easily within the mat.

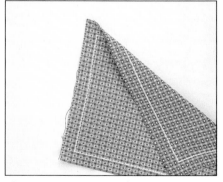

2 Using a zigzag stitch on your sewing machine sew a row of stitches 2.5cm/1in in from all four cut edges. This forms a tight edge and will allow you to fray the fabric up to this point.

Matching
Napkin Rings

I have designed these to match the place mats, but you could make them in contrasting colours and fabrics.

MATERIALS

fabric

matching thread

needle

scissors

napkin

Hints

You could use a contrasting thread in your sewing machine to form a coloured stitching seam for an informal look.

3 Use your fingers to tease out the horizontal threads around the edge of the mat. Remove all these threads until you have reached the stitched seam on all four sides. You will now have a beautifully soft, frayed border.

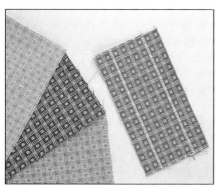

1 Roll up a napkin to give you the diameter of the ring. Add 4cm/ 1¾in seam allowance. The width of the ring should be 8cm/3¼in. To this measurement add 2.5cm/1in for the frayed edge to match the place mats. Using a zigzag stitch on your machine sew a row of stitches 2.5cm/1in in from the long, cut edges.

2 Use a straight stitch to sew the two narrow edges together to form a circle. Cut one edge of the seam close to its stitching line. Fold the second edge over by 1.25cm/½in. Fold this over the seam to enclose it. Hand stitch in place using a needle and thread.

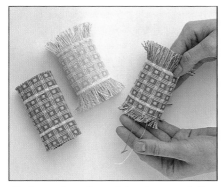

3 From the edge of the ring carefully tease out the threads until you have reached the row of stitches. You won't be able to pull any more threads beyond this point. Continue until the top and bottom edges of the napkin ring are frayed evenly.

135

Lacy Shelf Edging

As open shelving is so popular in country-style kitchens, this is an attractive way to finish the cottage look. Use glue or decoratively headed tacks to position the lacy edging on to your shelf or dresser

MATERIALS

PVA

household paint brush

plain fabric

plastic

pattern paper

scissors

tea cup/ruler

pencil

pinking scissors

fabric punch

1 Thin half a cup of PVA glue with an equal quantity of water. Use a household brush to paint this over one side of some plain fabric to stiffen. You will find it easier to put a layer of plastic underneath the fabric. When the fabric is dry this will simply peel off the stiffened cloth.

2 Cut a paper template using the curved rim of a teacup to form a scalloped edge or a ruler to make an easy zigzag shape. Draw your pattern onto the fabric, repeating it until your trim is long enough to fit your shelf. Cut out the edges using pinking scissors for a pretty lacy quality.

3 Draw a simple design on one of the shapes. Fold the shapes over one another, in a concertina fashion until you have a thickness of four or five. Use the fabric hole punch to form the pattern. Vary the size of the holes for a more interesting effect.

Fabric Primulas

These pots of flowers look fabulous, particularly if there are two or three grouped together. Show them off in a small bathroom where it is difficult to grow fresh plants.

MATERIALS

coloured acrylic paints

PVA

household paint brush

white cotton fabric

tracing paper

pencil

pattern paper

scissors

artist's paint brush

florist's wire

florist's tape

skewer

small flowerpot

florist's foam

sphagnum moss

Preparation

Select the coloured acrylic paints for the flowers. Mix half a cup of PVA glue with a 5cm/2in squeeze of the appropriate colour. Use a household brush to paint each colour onto a piece of white cotton fabric. Hang the fabric up to dry, preferably outside on a clothesline.

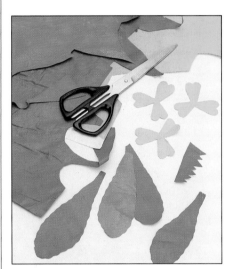

1 Copy our shapes to make paper templates of the petals, leaf and calyx. Cut two petal shapes for each flower from the yellow fabric and ten leaf shapes for each pot from the green fabric and one calyx for each flower from the green fabric.

2 Shade the centre of each petal shape with green acrylic paint. Different coloured flowers should have different shading. Paint faint white lines on the leaf shapes to represent the veins in the leaves.

3 Prepare the flower stems by wrapping a calyx around the top of the florist's wire, hold in place by binding with florist's tape. Keep the tape taut all the time overlapping it slightly as you twist it down the stem.

4 Pierce the centre of each petal with a skewer. Spread PVA on to the calyx and push two petals on the wire to surround this. Bind florist's wire to the leaf shapes with tape. Put flowers and leaves into a pot with dry florist's foam and cover with sphagnum moss.

Fruity Découpage Pelmet

This pretty scalloped edge flatters any window and could be used to disguise an unattractive curtain head or, positioned above the window frame, to make a smaller window appear larger.

MATERIALS

plywood or MDF

tape measure

saw

source material

watercolour paints

paintbrush

paper glue

glue brush

acrylic varnish

right-angled brackets

screws

Hints

Attach this pelmet to the wall using angled brackets. If the corners need boxing in, cut two smaller pieces from MDF or plywood and attach them to the front of the pelmet at right angles with strong wood glue, to form three sides of a rectangle.

1 Carefully cut a sheet of plywood or MDF to the size of the finished pelmet. Then make a suitably sized scallop shape and use this as a template to draw a scalloped edge along the bottom of the pelmet. Cut out the detached edge using a fret saw. Paint the surface with the base colour.

2 Cut out the images from their source book. Use a photocopier if you need to reproduce the same image several times and tint the images with watercolour paints. A simple wash should be all that is required.

3 Leave to dry and then attach the board to the angled brackets as described in Hints (opposite).

Mosaic Window Box

This ceramic mosaic is constructed from broken pieces of china. Scour secondhand shops and car boot sales for odd cups, saucers and plates.

MATERIALS

terracotta planter

china

newspaper/plastic bags

hammer

old spoon and knife

emulsion paint

grout/adhesive

rubber gloves (optional)

cloth

Hints

Place the china pieces in a plastic bag or between several sheets of newspaper, then tap sharply with a hammer. Remove the larger pieces and throw away the smaller ones.

1 Stir approximately two tablespoons of coloured emulsion paint into a quantity of tile adhesive/grout. Use an old spoon to mix the paste together. Mix small quantities at first, making more as you need it.

2 Use an old kitchen knife to spread a generous layer of tile adhesive/grout onto the rim of the planter. Select pieces of ceramic and push these firmly into the paste. Any sharp pieces that jut out can be tapped off later when the mosaic is set.

3 Working slowly down the sides of the planter. Apply the paste and press in the ceramic pieces, then apply more paste and continue until the planter is covered. Try to place straight edges of ceramic against the sides of the planter.

4 Leave the grout to stand for about an hour before using it to fill in the gaps between the ceramic pieces. Use your finger to do this (wear an old rubber glove if your skin is sensitive). Wipe excess grout from the surface with a damp cloth.

Buttonhole Pelmet

If your curtains lack interest or are in need of a lift, this pretty
pelmet idea is quick and simple to make.

MATERIALS

main fabric	pins
tape measure	buttonhole fabric
scissors	needle
sewing machine	brass rings
thread	brass hooks

Hints

The clever knotting at the sides of this pelmet make it very simple to remove for cleaning.
To attach the pelmet, you will need a simple brass ring screwed at each end of the window,
2.5cm/1in or so from the top of the frame.

1 Cut a rectangle from a double thickness of fabric. The width measures one-and-half-times the window's width, and the drop should be a quarter to a fifth of the window height. Allow 2.5cm/1in for turnings. With right sides together, stitch three sides, turn the right sides out and stitch the gap closed.

2 Sew small pieces of contrasting fabric 5 x 7.5cm/2 x 3in onto the wrong side of the pelmet only a fraction below the top hem, and approximately 15cm/6in apart. Sew a buttonhole in the centre of each rectangle and snip through all thicknesses. Push the fabric through the hole.

3 On the right side, hand sew the raw edges under on all four sides of the buttonhole facing. Make tiny stitches using a similarly coloured thread. You may need to tug the fabric slightly to stop the fabric bunching up at the top and bottom of the buttonhole. If this does not work you may need to re-snip the buttonhole.

4 Cut the tie from a double thickness of fabric, and along the fabric fold. The depth of the tie is 4cm/1 1/2in and the length equals the pelmet. Allow 2.5cm/1in for turnings. With right sides facing, sew along one end and the long side. Turn right sides out and stitch the open edge closed. Press flat, thread through the pelmet and tie.

Acetate Window Decoration

Children's bedroom windows - or kitchen windows - can be made to look more cheerful with these simple acetate stickers. Use waterproof pens or ink to colour in your design and simply stick them on the glass.

MATERIALS

self-adhesive plastic

scissors

chinagraph pencil

waterproof markers/inks

paintbrushes

Hints

Waterproof markers will glide on the plastic surface easily, but coloured inks will need a second coat for a more solid colour.

1 Cut a piece of self-adhesive plastic approximately to the size of the required design. Using a chinagraph pencil lightly draw in the design's details, or use the ink directly on the surface. Paint in the separate colours. Coloured ink may resist slightly, so paint on a second coat once the first is dry.

2 Use a black marker pen or black ink to draw an outline around the coloured design. You will need to use a fine artist's paintbrush if you are using fluid ink. Add vein detailing on the leaves. Leave to dry.

3 Cut the design from the sheet using a sharp pair of scissors. Follow the outline quite carefully, but allow an extra thickness of plastic around the narrow parts of the design to make application easier. Peel away the backing paper and stick the plastic to the window.

Shell Placemats

I used old wooden placemats for this project, but you could make them from cork or even thick cardboard.

MATERIALS

place mats

spray paint

shell patterned paper

scissors

plasticine

PVA glue

varnish

Hints

It is possible to use oil-based paint to cover the place mats but allow a longer drying time.

1 Cover the surface of the old placemats using the spray paint. You may find that you need several coats to obliterate all the design underneath. Spray the paint evenly, building up thin layers and allowing it to dry between coats.

2 Cut out the shells from the paper. If you cannot find a shell paper, fish or fruit prints cut from wrapping paper or magazines would look just as effective. Position the shells on the mat securing with plasticine until you are happy with the arrangement.

3 Remove the plasticine and glue the shells onto the place mat using PVA glue. Leave to dry then seal and protect with at least three layers of varnish. Repeat until you have completed all the placemats. Remember these are wipe-clean only.

Blind Trim

This is a wonderful way of jazzing up your existing plain blind for a small cost. Simply sew the strip down the centre of the blind.

MATERIALS

fabric – main border

fabric – coloured strip

scissors

thread

iron-on decoration

Hints

An open weave fabric is ideal for this treatment as it will fringe very easily.

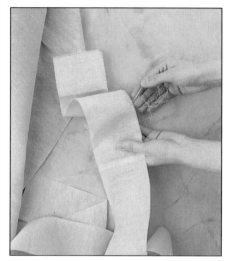

1 Cut strips of fabric, 7.5cm/3in wide, to form the border. Sew strips together, if necessary, to achieve the same length as your blind. Allow 4cm/1¾in for the turnings at the top and bottom. On each of the long edges tease out the threads to give a softly frayed border.

2 Cut the coloured fabric for the centre strips. These should measure 7.5cm/3in including turnings. Join strips if necessary. Fold the fabric over and sew a seam down the length 1.25cm/½in from the edge. Trim the seam and press. Turn right side out.

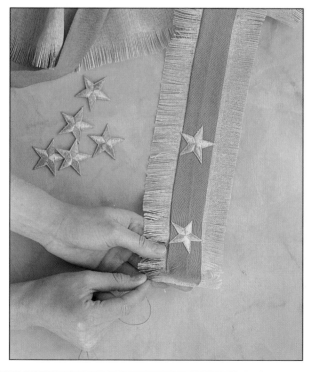

3 Sew the fabric piece to the centre of the border down both sides, using a straight stitch. Apply your decoration. I have used iron-on gold stars but you could use anything from tiny shells to pretty buttons or beads. Sew to centre of the blind.

Biscuit Barrel

This is a fascinating way of using a colour photocopier and gives an attractive finish to a simple container.

MATERIALS

scissors

handmade paper

wooden storage container

real flowers

photocopied print

PVA glue

emulsion paint

household paint brush

spray varnish

Hints

You could place any flower on the photocopier but choose one with an intense colour such as this cornflower.

1 Cut a piece of handmade paper to cover one side of the barrel. Mine has eight sides but yours may have more or less, it doesn't matter. Place your chosen flower in the centre of the paper. Colour photocopy this as many times as you have sides on your box.

2 Cut around the copied print and glue the image onto the container using the PVA glue. Smooth out any air bubbles that may appear under the surface. Continue applying the prints in this way until you have covered the container.

3 Paint the lid of the barrel an appropriate shade, using the emulsion paint. You will probably need two coats for good coverage. When completely dry, use a spray varnish to seal and protect the finished container.

Knotted Buttonhole Tiebacks

Tiebacks are without a doubt extremely useful. They can, however, look quite boring in their conventional form so here is a unique approach to tying back your curtains.

MATERIALS

tape measure

paper

pencil

scissors

triangle fabric

thread

sewing machine

iron and ironing board

tieback fabric

needle

brass rings

brass hooks

Hints

For more traditional curtains use the same fabric for the tiebacks as for the curtains. However, if your room warrants it, go for an eclectic look: mismatched checks or a selection of muted floral chintzes would each look exciting.

To make a template for your tiebacks, pass a cloth tape measure around your curtains at the point where the tiebacks will be to determine its length. Transfer this measurement onto paper, and then draw a crescent shape around the line using the tieback featured on this page as a guide. Cut out the resulting shape.

1 For each tieback, cut small triangles from a double thickness of fabric. Two sides of the triangle should measure 9cm/3 $\frac{1}{2}$in and the base approximately 7.5cm/3in. Stitch down the two longer sides leaving a seam allowance of 12mm/$\frac{1}{2}$in, turn the shape to the right side and press flat using a steam iron.

2 Use the paper template described in the Hints text to the left to cut two crescent shapes from the main fabric. Place them together with right sides facing and insert the triangles along the bottom edge, points facing into the crescent tieback. Stitch around the edges, leaving a seam allowance of 12mm/$\frac{1}{2}$in. Leave a small gap to turn the tieback to the right side. Stitch the gap closed.

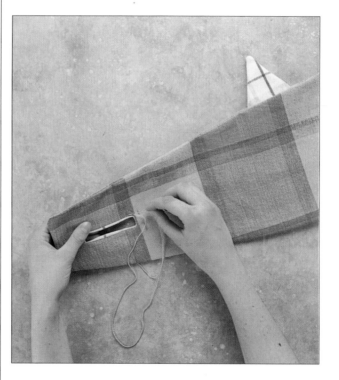

3 Place a rectangle of fabric cut from that used for the triangles over one end of the tieback and stitch a 4cm/1 $\frac{1}{2}$in buttonhole over this. Snip the buttonhole and push the fabric through to the other side. Hand sew the buttonhole flat on the right side, and turn under the raw edges on the reverse. To attach the tiebacks onto hooks fixed to the wall, stitch a small brass ring to the centre of each tieback on the wrong side. Scoop each curtain into a tieback and slip the tie through the buttonhole.

BEDROOM PROJECTS

Stylish draping and clever fabric techniques will certainly introduce style to your bedroom. For a touch of glamour and sophistication, try the bed corona on page 192 or the decorative folding screen on page 174. Classic designs such as the Bloomsbury-style painted cupboard on page 172 or the striking tartan tallboy on page 168 look impressive, but are actually very easy to create. The key to affordable luxury is often in the accessories you choose – use small amounts of sumptuous fabrics and tassels or fabric tie-backs, such as those on pages 158 and 198 for a really stunning effect.

For the more traditional amongst you, furniture can be treated with crackle glaze for an instant antiquated finish. Try creating the classic headboard on page 180 or adapting the wonderful *trompe l'oeil* Venetian villa drawers on page 164 to one of your own designs. Frame and drape your windows in the softest sheer fabrics as on page 166 and top them with the punched pelmet on page 194 to create a secluded haven away from the rest of the busy world.

Patchwork Bed Cover

This is patchwork at its simplest and yet it gives a beautiful decorative look to an otherwise plain bed cover.

MATERIALS

fabric -main

fabric – check and plain

pattern paper

thread

scissors

pins

Hints

Use your mattress measurements to cut your fabric. The cover should be measured lengthways, from just under the pillows to the base of the divan and widthways, at the bottom edge of the divan from one side to the other.

Preparation

Cut two rectangles from your main fabric. The rectangle for the top of the cover will be 15cm/6in smaller all round than the bottom. Add a seam allowance of 1.25cm/½in for the three sides and a 7.5cm/3in hem for the top edge. This will be the opening edge.

1 Cut 15cm/6in patchwork squares in both the checked and plain fabrics. Sew these together alternately to form three border strips. Turn under all the raw edges. Pin one strip to the base edge of your top cover. Then pin on the two sides to co-ordinate with this. Sew in place.

2 Use the pattern paper to cut a template 15 x 10 cm/6 x 4in for the trims. Shape as shown.Cut out trims in a double thickness of both checked and plain fabrics. Allow for turnings. Place two trim pieces right sides together and sew around the curved edges. Turn right sides out and press. Repeat with the remaining trim pieces.

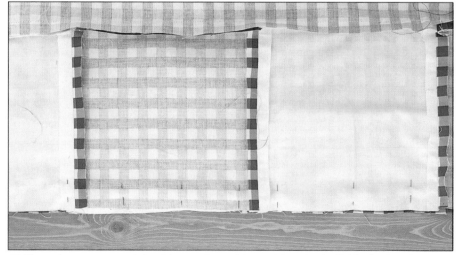

3 Place the top cover right side up. Over this position the individual trim pieces right sides facing, alternating the positions of the blue and white fabric.Pin and stitch. Turn the cover to the right side out and press the trim edge flat. Turn under the allowance for the hem along the top of the cover. Cut a 10cm/4in wide gingham strip to this length. Right sides facing pin then sew one long edge to the top of the cover. Fold over the gingham to cover the seam and hand sew in position.

Beachcomber Tiebacks

Any shells or attractive pebbles would look good decorating this tieback. I have even added corks and driftwood for a truly "beachcomber" look.

MATERIALS

paper ribbon in various colours

scissors

crepe paper

string

florist's wire

pliers

small terracotta plant pots

drill and bit

shells

corks

driftwood

pebbles

raffia

Hints

Twist a piece of wire to the centre of each string loop to make it easier to push this through the terracotta plant pots.

1 Cut at least four strips of paper ribbon into 1m/40in lengths and tease the crinkled paper out with your fingers. Cut similar lengths from the crepe paper. Additional lengths of ribbon and paper will make a wider tieback.

2 Cut three 145cm/57in lengths of string and plait together. Plait together all the paper and ribbon strips. Twist a piece of wire with the extra length of string and fold to form a loop. Push each loop through a plant pot.

3 Drill small holes through all the shells, corks, wood and pebbles to be strung. Any difficult items can be held in a cradle of raffia, knotted on both sides of the item. Attach all the decorations to the tiebacks with raffia, making sure they will hang across the front of the curtain.

Decorated Drawers

I used pictures torn from an old diary for these drawers but if you want to use pictures from a book simply colour-photocopy the images instead.

MATERIALS

coloured pictures

craft knife

painted drawers

PVA glue

watercolour paint

white emulsion paint

household paint brush

wire wool

Hints

Instead of bird images you could choose pictures that represent the contents of the drawers - toys for a child's room, tools or sewing materials for practical use, even make-up or jewellery for the dressing table.

1 Assemble the pictures to be used. I collected as many bird images as I could to cover the front panels of these drawers. It's probably better to cut out more images than you think you will need so you can make a collage of the pieces.

2 Cut out the images neatly with the craft knife. Arrange on the drawer fronts until you are satisfied with the design. You may need to remove some or all of the drawer knobs. When you are satisfied with the design glue the pictures with PVA.

3 To make the cut images blend with the painted surface, mix a little watercolour with white emulsion until you have a colour close to that on the drawers. Paint this sparingly over the pictures. Rub away some of the wet paint with wire wool to add further detail.

Chair/Bed Throw

This throw is warm and comforting with its layer of interlining. Toss it over a bed or an armchair for casual style.

MATERIALS

fabric – top

fabric – lining

interlining

pins

thread

scissors

Hints

Because you are dealing with large pieces of fabric, it may be helpful to tack the layers together, before sewing. Use long stitches which can be removed after the final sewing.

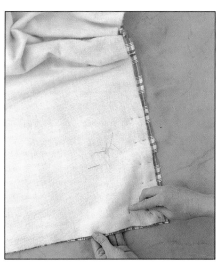

1 Cut top fabric and interlining to fit the top of a single or double bed. Pin and sew the interlining to the wrong side of the fabric. Use a straight stitch and machine approximately 1.25cm/½in from the raw edges.

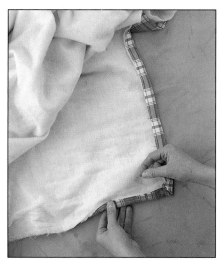

2 Turn the sewn edge over the interlining by 2.5cm/1in, then pin and sew this edge to form a narrow hem all the way around the throw. As this is very narrow keep your stitching lines as close to the turned edge as possible.

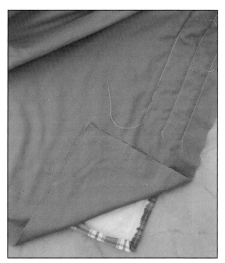

3 Cut the lining 7.5cm/3in larger all around. Pin, then sew to the interlined fabric. The excess is to be frayed later. Sew a row of stitches close to the fabric edge. For added detail sew two more rows 5cm/2in apart, towards the centre of the throw.

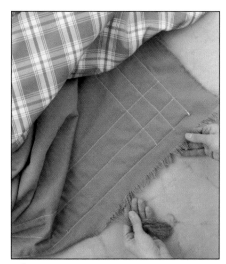

4 Pull out the threads on the excess lining fabric to fray the border. Because the throw is quite large this will take some time but it is well worth the effort. Pull the threads as far as the first stitching line.

Trompe l'oeil Venetian Villa Drawers

This clever design was inspired by the brilliant style of marquetry that was popular at the turn of the century.

MATERIALS

white acrylic primer

white emulsion – base coat

coloured emulsion paint – top coat

emulsion glaze

acrylic artists' paints

low tack masking tape

ruler

pencil

artists' brushes

paint kettle

paint brush

sandpaper

Hints

If a Venetian villa isn't quite your style, look at pictures of alternative architectural designs for inspiration.

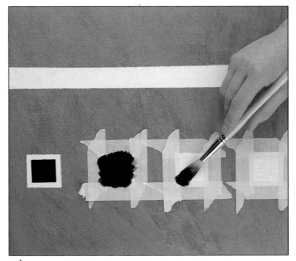

1 Remove any knobs or handles from your set of drawers. Prepare the surface for painting by applying the primer and one coat of the base coat. Sand down between each coat.

2 Mix equal quantities of glaze with the coloured emulsion top coat in a paint kettle. Add a little dark brown artist's acrylic paint to give depth to the terracotta colour. Apply to the surface with random circular movements to give a cloudy effect.

3 Using a pencil and ruler copy the positions of the windows and doors on the front of the drawers. Apply masking tape to the outside edges of these pencil marks. Paint the areas within the tape using cream artist's paint. When dry remove masking tape very carefully.

4 Use low tack masking tape to define the smaller areas within the window and door shapes. Paint with brown artist's paint inside these masked areas. Leave to dry, then remove the tape. For real authenticity add doors and windows to the sides of the chest.

Three Sheer Window Dressing

This is an ideal way to cover a small window. It is not designed to be drawn open but the sheer fabric filters the light, while the beads and gold thread sparkle for a very pretty effect.

MATERIALS

organza fabric

sheer fabric

shiny fabric

gold thread

card

sewing thread

needle

glass beads

pearls

dowelling

Hints

Secure the dowelling rods to the wooden architrave around the window, use light-weight brass fittings especially designed for curtain rods.

166

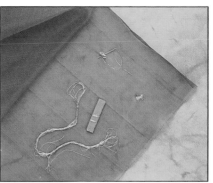

1 Cut all three fabrics to the size of your window. Add 2.5cm/1in to each side for turnings and 7.5cm/3in to the top edge to make a channel heading for dowelling. Allow 2.5cm/1in along the bottom edge for a hem.

2 To decorate the organza, wind gold thread approximately ten times around a small piece of card. Slip it off the card and use more gold thread to tie a knot around the middle to make a tiny bow. Repeat this until you have enough bows to stitch at random all over the fabric.

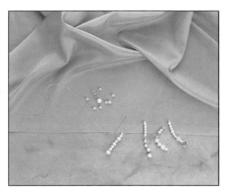

3 The second silky fabric has a beaded decorative edge. For this I re-strung small beads from old necklaces. Use pearls and glass beads for a pretty effect. Make the bead lengths about 5cm/2in long. Sew these to the bottom edge of the fabric after hemming.

4 I have sewn small individual pearls onto the third piece of fabric but you could use any type of beads. Glass ones look good but be careful not to use very large ones as they will pull the fabric and spoil the final display.

5 Sew all the side seams and bottom hems. The fabric with the beaded hem should be the same length (including beads) as the other two. Make any adjustments at the top edge. Fold over seam allowance at top edge and sew down. 2.5cm/1in above this sew another row of stitches to form the casing for the dowelling.

Tartan Tallboy

Tartan is popular so be adventurous and paint this striking design over your dullest pieces of furniture – it's bound to make a sensational transformation!

MATERIALS

white acrylic primer

coloured emulsion paint – base coat

5 coloured emulsion paints – for tartan effect

fine artist's brushes

pencil

masking tape

sandpaper

ruler

Preparation

This is a good paint technique to use on a battered old tallboy as the patterning conceals any defects. Prepare old drawers by sanding thoroughly, then apply the acrylic primer. Paint with two coats of the coloured emulsion base coat.

Hints

You will find it easier to paint your tallboy in stages. Begin with the frame and then the drawers. If the prospect is too daunting, paint the drawers only.

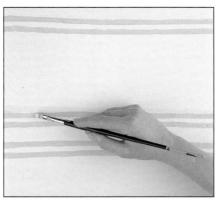

1 Decide where you want your tartan pattern to be painted and mark out the first lines using a pencil and ruler. The first colour is applied as parallel lines with a 2.5cm/1in gap between and a 15cm/6in space between the sets of parallel lines.

2 Apply the second colour, again in parallel lines, but this time paint them vertically so they cross through the previously painted lines. You may now feel more confident about painting free hand, but I don't think it really matters if the lines are wobbly.

3 Apply the third colour, again vertically, in the middle of the 15cm/6in gap. I drew one thick line with a fine line on each side, but choose whatever style of lines you prefer.

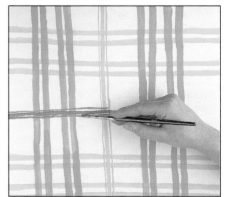

4 Use a slightly darker shade of the previous colour to reproduce a similar trio of horizontal lines. Again these should be painted within the 15cm/6in gap left in step 1.

Tartan Door Knobs

This really is a clever way of adding decoration to your drawers or cupboards, especially if you can't face the all-over tartan effect.

MATERIALS

white acrylic primer

coloured emulsion paint – base coat

coloured emulsion paints – for tartan

fine artist's brushes

polyurethane varnish

Hints

Knobs are always tricky to paint on a flat surface so you may find it easier to insert a long screw into the base of each to provide a handle. Support on a bottle while drying.

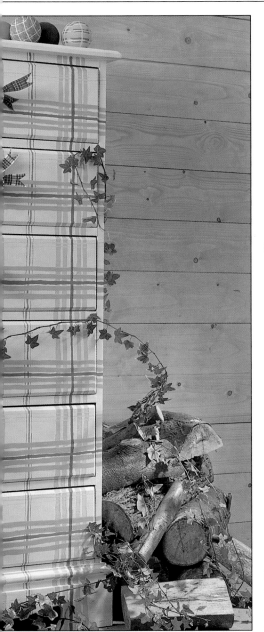

1 Prepare your knobs by priming them, then apply one coat of base coat. This base coat colour can either match or contrast with the colour of the drawers or cupboard for which the knobs are intended.

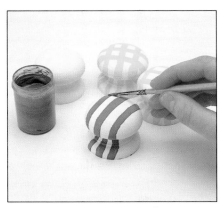

2 With small objects it really isn't necessary to use masking tape as a guide but it may be better to plan the tartan lines in pencil on your first knob. Paint on thick lines horizontally and vertically to form a chessboard effect.

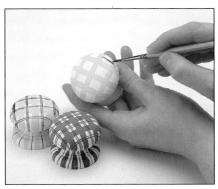

3 Paint a fine double line horizontally and vertically through the centre of the chequered pattern to produce a simple tartan effect. Leave to dry and finish with one layer of varnish.

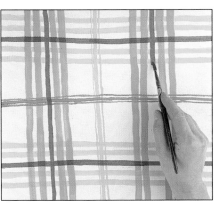

5 The final lines are painted in the boldest colour of all and are positioned within the 2.5cm/1in gap of the original vertical and horizontal lines.

Antiqued Wardrobe

This is a very distinctive technique to give an ordinary wooden wardrobe an aged look that could fool generations to come.

MATERIALS

white acrylic primer

coloured emulsion paint – base coat

crackle glaze

coloured emulsion paint – top coat

sanding block

sandpaper

wire wool

artist's acrylic paint – burnt umber

paint brush

paint kettle

Hints

The colours of the base and top coats should always contrast to give a strong final effect.

1 Prepare the wardrobe by first applying the primer and then the base coat. It's a good idea to sand down between coats to achieve a smooth finish. If the wardrobe is secondhand you may need to vacuum the inside.

2 When the paint is dry, apply a thin layer of crackle glaze to the wardrobe. I decided to crackle glaze just the panels to emphasise their shape and give them a distinctive look. Allow to dry.

3 Apply the coloured emulsion paint top coat to the remainder of the wardrobe, then finally to the panels. Work quickly over the panels. The paint will interact with the glaze and start to crack very quickly.

4 When the emulsion top coat on the remainder of the wardrobe is dry, use the sanding block to rub away small areas to give the effect of wear. I decided to sand areas of the centre panel as well, but this is not essential.

5 Dilute the raw umber artist's paint with water in a small paint kettle. Dip the wire wool into the paint and rub over the wardrobe to remove further patches of emulsion. This leaves an attractive overall tinted colour.

Stylised Painted Cupboard

This cupboard has a regular pattern that is remarkably easy to paint. You could enlarge the scale and paint the same design over your walls as a brighter alternative to paper.

MATERIALS

white acrylic primer

coloured emulsion paint – base coat

3 colours emulsion paint – for pattern

fine artist's brush

paint brush

tracing paper

thin cardboard

pencil

Hints

Any stylised leaf shape would look good in this pattern. Experiment with a few alternatives before you commit yourself.

1 Prime and base coat the cupboard. You'll find it easier to paint furniture with legs if you turn the piece upside down and paint the legs first before painting the rest.

2 If you want to copy my simple leaf design trace the outline from this page. Use this to make a cardboard template and draw at random all over your cupboard. Infill this outline with boldly coloured emulsion paint.

3 Trace the central oak leaf shape again from this page and make a second card template. Position within the original leaf shape and draw around. Infill with a lighter shade of emulsion paint.

4 The final fanciful detail on my cup-board uses a contrasting colour and is a simple curved outline created with a quick sweeping freehand movement of the brush.

Folding Screen

Once popular at the turn of the century, screens are now enjoying a decorative comeback.

MATERIALS

fabric

cotton interfacing

PVA

scissors

pattern paper

Hints

Clip the hem allowance to make it easier to fold the fabric evenly over the curved areas. Use undiluted PVA at the edges for a stronger bonding.

1 Separate the panels of the screen remembering the position of the hinges. Use each panel as a template for the fabric panels. Cut fabric for each screen panel, front and back. Add at least a 2.5cm/1in turning allowance around all the sides.

2 Unless your screen is white, any other colour may show through. If so back the fabric with a layer of cotton interfacing. Cut out the iron-on interfacing using the cut fabric pieces as templates. Use a hot iron to fuse the interfacing onto the fabric.

3 Thin the PVA glue with an equal quantity of water and apply to each panel. Stick the fabric in place on each panel, pressing from the centre outwards in all directions, to avoid any air bubbles. Turn over and glue down edges. Back the screen with complementary or contrasting fabric.

Fabric-covered Pelmet

Using MDF (medium-density fibreboard) you can create any shape of pelmet you wish, from a simple scalloped shape like mine to something curved and fanciful.

MATERIALS

pattern paper

scissors

wadding

fabric – patterned

fabric – white

PVA

curved needle

thread

wooden beads

emulsion paint

paint brush

all-purpose adhesive

Hints

You can use ribbon for your gathered trim. Any ribbon would work provided it is wide enough for the two lines of gathering stitches.

1 Make a paper template of the pelmet. Cut wadding to the same size. Stick the wadding to the pelmet with PVA glue. When the fabric is stretched over the edges it will flatten the wadding and this will soften the hard edges of the pelmet.

2 Cut the fabric to fit the pelmet allowing 2.5cm/1in extra all round for turnings. Cut notches in the edges of the fabric so it will fit around the curves easily. Glue excess to the back. Cover the back of the pelmet folding in the turnings and gluing down for a neat finish.

3 Cut 5cm/2 in wide strips from the white fabric, join if necessary until it measures twice the length of the pelmet. Sew two rows of long stitches, 1.25cm/$\frac{1}{2}$in from each edge. Pull up to gather the trim.

4 Use a curved needle to sew the gathered trim to the pelmet. Sew a row of stitches down the middle of the trimming. Catch plenty of the wadding with each stitch as the trimming needs to lie flat against the pelmet.

5 As an optional extra you can paint wooden beads with emulsion paint and secure with adhesive, at intervals along the gathered trim.

Tented Wardrobe

This wardrobe is created by extending the top shelf and giving it a slightly curved edge. The tented top section will overlap this. Fix a curtain track to the front edge of the shelf.

MATERIALS

cup hook

tape measure

pattern paper

scissors

buckram

fabric

piping cord

contrasting fabric

dinner plate

heading tape

thread

cleat

brass ring

curtain track

curtain hooks

curved shelf

Hints

Screw a hook into the ceiling centrally above the wardrobe. Use a metal tape to measure the height and width of the tent area. Divide the width into equal parts to give you the number of tent sections.

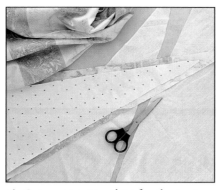

1 Cut a paper template for the tent section. Use to cut out the buckram sections as a backing first and then cut the fabric pieces. Allow 1.25cm/½in all round the fabric for turnings. Sew fabric to buckram with straight stitch close to the edges.

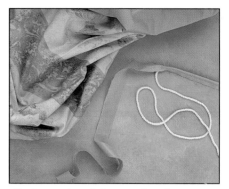

2 Cover the piping cord with contrasting fabric. Use a tape measure to calculate the amount of piping you'll need, remember to include the piping across the bottom of each section.

3 Sew all the tent sections together inserting the piping between each section. Turn the top ends of the piping neatly over to the reverse side where they meet at the pointed top of the tent.

4 Use a dinner plate to make a template for a scalloped border. Cut out in buckram and fabric. To join buckram and fabric, sew around the scalloped edge. Sew the top edge of the border to the tented section again sewing piping cord between.

5 Make an unlined curtain for the wardrobe. Measure the drop, and 1½ times the width. Add 2.5cm/1in for the bottom hem and 5cm/2in for the heading. Also add a 2.5cm/1in seam allowance down either side. Cut the curtain and sew down the allowances.

6 Sew the heading tape to the top of the curtain and pull in the gathers, secure to a cleat and use curtain hooks to hang the curtain. Sew a ring to the top of the tented section and hook onto the ceiling. Pull the tented area over the shelf and heading tape.

Classic Headboard

The beauty of cutting your own headboard is that you can create any shape you like, from a classic arch to something curved and fanciful.

MATERIALS

MDF (medium density fibreboard)

wadding

PVA

fabric – headboard

fabric – border

fabric – piping

piping cord

sewing pins

thread

pencil

ruler

scissors

staple gun

needle

Hints

I have cut a new shape for my headboard using MDF, but you could recover an old headboard simply by removing the old fabric.

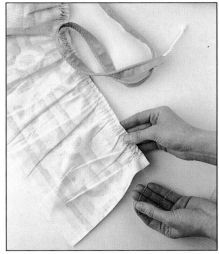

1 Position the wadding over the headboard and cut out. Don't worry about cutting this to cover the sides of the headboard, because when you cover it with the fabric the wadding will be pulled over the edges enough to soften them. Use a little PVA to stick the wadding to the front of the headboard.

2 Lay the headboard on a flat surface – the floor is probably the easiest place. Put the fabric over the wadding. Take time to position it carefully and match the pattern with the shape of the headboard. If you are using fabric with an obvious stripe or check make sure this is perfectly square and the lines on the pattern are parallel.

3 Cut a 20cm/8in wide border from the fabric. This should be one and a half times the length of the headboard edge. Sew two lines of stitches on one of the longest edges. Pull these threads to gather the fabric. Using a contrasting fabric cover two lengths of piping cord. Sew to ruched edge of the border allowing more fullness where it bends round a curve.

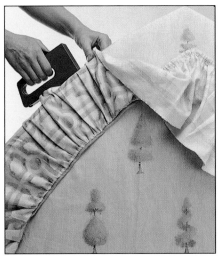

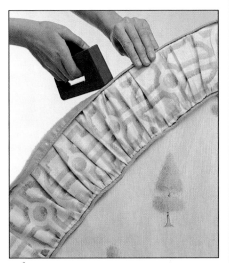

4 Use a pencil and ruler to mark the position of the border on the headboard about 18cm/7in in from the outer edge. Place the border right side down on the headboard so its seam matches the pencilled line. Pin in place. Turn border over and check its position. Staple in place, or use a curved needle to sew the border securely to the headboard fabric.

5 Pull the remaining edge of the border taut and staple to the back of the headboard. Cover another length of piping cord with a contrasting fabric to fit around this outer edge.

6 Take the second length of covered piping cord and staple or use a curved needle to sew the top edge of the headboard. To finish, roll the piping back slightly with your fingers and using tiny stitches sew down to hide the row of staples or stitches.

Director's Chair Cover

This lovely slip-over cover transforms the boring old director's chair so it can be used anywhere in the home.

MATERIALS

3 patterned fabrics

pattern paper

scissors

pins

thread

Hints

Make a simple cushion cover from any scraps of fabric that may be left after covering your chair.

1 I have chosen three different fabrics for my director's chair. They are all linked by colour, in this case pale yellow and by design, as all three fabrics have a rose featured in their pattern.

2 Cut pattern paper templates to the dimensions of the director's chair. I find it easier to lay the paper over the chair and cut while in place. When you cut the fabric add 1.25cm/½in all round for seam allowance. Use a zigzag stitch over the raw edges to stop the fabric from fraying.

3 I used: one long piece from the front hem over the seat and backrest to the lower hem; 2 outside pieces; 2 inside pieces; 1 strip over the armrest; 1 strip between the front and back of the backrest. Pin, then sew the pieces together. Turn up the hem, take care when you sew in the corners of the chair. Press each seam open before progressing. Clip the seams where necessary particularly at corners such as these armrests. Turn the cover to the right side and slip over the chair.

Scallop-edged Duvet Cover

Duvet covers are very easy to sew and can be decorated with all sorts of trimmings. The scalloped edge gives a neat tailored look to an otherwise plain cover. Use a clean dustbin lid as a guide for the curves.

MATERIALS

3 contrasting fabrics

scissors

dustbin lid

pins

press studs

needle

thread

Hints

If your fabric is not wide enough for the required width of the duvet, join side strips to a central panel for a more professional finish.

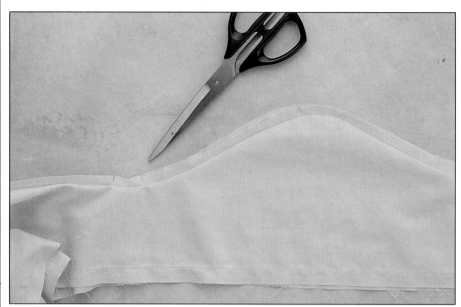

1 Cut two pieces of fabric to fit your duvet add 1.25cm/½in seam allowance on three sides and 5cm/2in for a deeper hem at the opening on the top edge. Cut 2 scallop-edged borders 15cm/6in wide to fit two sides and bottom edge of the duvet. Allow 10cm/4in extra for gathering around the corners. Right sides facing sew the scalloped edges together. Turn right side out.

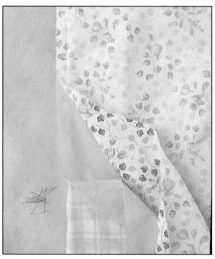

2 Turn under the allowance at the opening to form a double hem, pin then sew in place. Place the right sides of fabric together and sandwich the scalloped edge in between so all the raw edges are even. Pin, then sew in place.

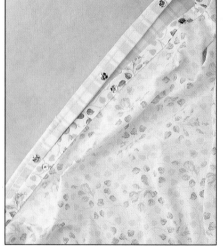

3 Sew large press studs at regular intervals across the opening. Turn the duvet right side out and pull the corners to even out the gathers.

Dressing Table

The traditional kidney-shaped dressing table has been given a new lease of life with this beautiful fresh floral print.

MATERIALS

tape measure

fabric

curtain heading tape

pattern paper

scissors

pins

lining

interfacing

piping cord

contrasting fabric

needle

thread

pearl drops

Hints

I have scalloped the border of this dressing table for a pretty edge.

1 Make the skirt section first. Measure the depth of the dressing table and one and a half times the track for the width. Allow an extra 15cm/6in for the front overlap and 1.25cm/½in for turnings. Sew the hem and the side seams. Sew the heading tape to cover the raw edges along the top of the skirt.

2 Cut pattern paper to fit the table top plus 1.25cm/½in for turnings. Pin to fabric and cut. Cut a fabric and lining border to fit top, 15cm/6in deep plus turnings. Cut a strip of iron-on interfacing to this size less the seam allowance. Iron to the fabric border.

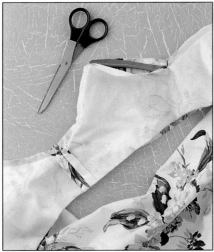

3 Cover piping cord to fit around the table top and border. Right sides facing sandwich the piping cord between border and lining around scalloped edge. Turn right side out. Sandwich more piping between cover top and border, sew together.

4 Cover another length of piping cord to go around the hem of the dressing table skirt. Right sides facing pin then sew in place. Sew on the pearl drops to border edge.

Découpaged Headboard

I have used offcuts from rolls of wallpaper to make this découpage headboard. Look for faded ochre and sepia colours for a more romantic feel.

MATERIALS

headboard

wallpaper offcuts

scissors

wallpaper paste

household paint brush

PVA glue

varnish

Hints

Strip any fabric from your old headboard and decorate with emulsion paint. Or cut a new headboard from MDF, paint, then transfer the fittings from the old headboard.

1 Cut out all the large groups of flowers and the largest individual flowers from the wallpaper. Position on the headboard, moving them around until you have a pleasing arrangement. Don't worry about gaps, these can be filled in later. Paste the shapes down.

2 Cut out the smaller individual flowers and leaves and paste these into the gaps. Use PVA glue on those flowers that need to overlap the already pasted flowers, for a more permanent bonding. You may find you need lots of these smaller pieces.

3 Cut out all the finer detailed pieces of the wallpaper like buds and leaf stems. This may seem quite tedious and time consuming, but the end result is worth it. Stick these all around the headboard filling in the gaps. Protect with two or three layers of varnish.

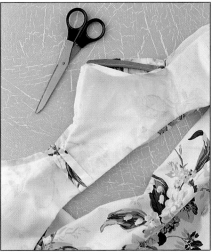

1 Make the skirt section first. Measure the depth of the dressing table and one and a half times the track for the width. Allow an extra 15cm/6in for the front overlap and 1.25cm/½in for turnings. Sew the hem and the side seams. Sew the heading tape to cover the raw edges along the top of the skirt.

2 Cut pattern paper to fit the table top plus 1.25cm/½in for turnings. Pin to fabric and cut. Cut a fabric and lining border to fit top, 15cm/6in deep plus turnings. Cut a strip of iron-on interfacing to this size less the seam allowance. Iron to the fabric border.

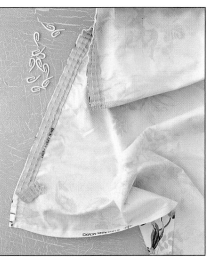

3 Cover piping cord to fit around the table top and border. Right sides facing sandwich the piping cord between border and lining around scalloped edge. Turn right side out. Sandwich more piping between cover top and border, sew together.

4 Cover another length of piping cord to go around the hem of the dressing table skirt. Right sides facing pin then sew in place. Sew on the pearl drops to border edge.

Photocopied Cherub Bedside Cabinets

For the true romantics this is a lovely way to decorate plain bedside cabinets. The photocopies form the outline for the painted cherubs but the effect looks like an original hand drawing.

MATERIALS

white acrylic primer

3 colours of emulsion paint – base coat

artist's acrylic paints

artist's brush

photocopies of cherubs

PVA glue

paint kettle

masking tape

scissors

Preparation

Prime the bedside cabinets and allow to dry. Mix equal quantities of one emulsion paint base coat with water in a paint kettle and apply to the body of each cabinet.

Hints

If you are decorating a child's room, painted photocopies of animals, clowns or their favourite heroes would be an inspired alternative to stencils. Don't be afraid to use a strong shade when colourwashing because the final result will be much paler.

1 Mark a 2.5cm/1in border around the edge of each cabinet door using masking tape. Mix equal quantities of the second emulsion base coat with water and apply to the central section within the masked area. You can use either a lighter variation of the first colour or a contrasting shade.

2 Remove the masking tape and reposition to protect the painted panel area. Paint the revealed border with the third emulsion paint colour, again mixed with an equal quantity of water. When removing masking tape avoid peeling away any layers of paint.

3 Cut out the cherub shapes from the photocopies and using the PVA glue position on the bedside cabinets. My cherubs were enlarged to fit neatly within the central panel of the cabinet door fronts.

4 Use the acrylic paints to colour the cherubs. At this stage you can let your imagination go wild with the colours. Or if you prefer, just leave the cherubs perfectly plain.

Découpaged Headboard

I have used offcuts from rolls of wallpaper to make this découpage headboard. Look for faded ochre and sepia colours for a more romantic feel.

MATERIALS

headboard

wallpaper offcuts

scissors

wallpaper paste

household paint brush

PVA glue

varnish

Hints

Strip any fabric from your old headboard and decorate with emulsion paint. Or cut a new headboard from MDF, paint, then transfer the fittings from the old headboard.

1 Cut out all the large groups of flowers and the largest individual flowers from the wallpaper. Position on the headboard, moving them around until you have a pleasing arrangement. Don't worry about gaps, these can be filled in later. Paste the shapes down.

2 Cut out the smaller individual flowers and leaves and paste these into the gaps. Use PVA glue on those flowers that need to overlap the already pasted flowers, for a more permanent bonding. You may find you need lots of these smaller pieces.

3 Cut out all the finer detailed pieces of the wallpaper like buds and leaf stems. This may seem quite tedious and time consuming, but the end result is worth it. Stick these all around the headboard filling in the gaps. Protect with two or three layers of varnish.

Bed Corona

Any shape can be sculpted around a basic half circle but this charming crown would be ideal for a little girl's bedroom. Secure the corona to the wall with L-shaped angle brackets.

MATERIALS

MDF (medium density fibreboard)

saw

tape measure

ruler

felt tip pen

cardboard

craft knife

staple gun/glue

paper strips

wallpaper paste

scissors

coloured paper

star wrapping paper

PVA glue

screw hooks

L-shaped brackets

Hints

The mosaic squares can be cut from any paper - coloured sweet wrappers would create a jewelled look.

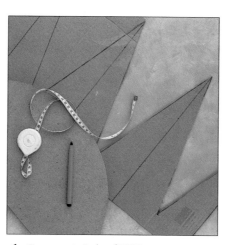

1 Cut a semi-circle of MDF approx 60cm/2ft diameter. Use a ruler to draw the pointed crown shape on card to this width. Each point should have a base measurement of approx 30cm/12in. Create half points on the outer edges. Using a craft knife cut out the crown shape.

2 Staple or glue the base of the crown to the edge of the MDF so the points face downwards. Stick torn strips of paper over the shape with wallpaper paste. Allow the first layer to dry before applying the next layer in the opposite direction. Apply at least five layers.

3 Cut tiny squares of coloured paper and glue to the crown with wallpaper paste in a mosaic fashion. Cut stars from wrapping paper and glue at random over the crown to complete the look. Screw hooks, 7.5cm/3in apart, under the rim of the corona to hold the curtain.

Punched Pelmet

This pelmet looks particularly attractive when positioned above a thin voile curtain so that the light diffuses through the fine material and its tiny pinprick holes.

MATERIALS

fusible buckram

scissors

pelmet fabric

tape measure

iron and ironing board

tracing paper

pencil

paper

darning needle

hammer

nail

staple gun

ribbon

fabric glue

Hints

In a small window where there is no need for curtains, use this punched pelmet on a reduced scale to add a decorative detail. Staple or tack the pelmet onto a pelmet board and cover the line of staples with a length of ribbon.

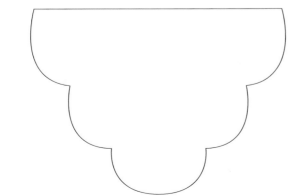

1 Cut the fusible buckram to the exact size required for your window. Cut plain cotton fabric to this size plus 2.5cm/1in all around for turning. Fuse the buckram onto the cotton with a hot iron, turning under the allowances. Trace the outline on this page and enlarge it on a photocopier to an appropriate size. Cut a template from the outline and use it to draw the motif along the bottom of the buckram pelmet. Cut out the design with scissors.

2 Copy the dots from the outline on this page onto the template and then position the template over the detailed edge. Push a darning needle through the dots as a guide for the punched holes. Then place the detailed edge against a piece of wood and use a hammer and nail to punch out the holes. Staple the pelmet to a board above the window frame and disguise the staples by gluing a ribbon over them.

Rose-covered Box

I love the simplicity of this patterned jewellery box. The whole design is cut from one sheet of wrapping paper with all its elements rearranged.

MATERIALS

wrapping paper

scissors

wooden box

emulsion paint

household paint brush

PVA glue

craft knife

varnish

Hints

Look through seed catalogues or gardening magazines for other designs to pattern your box.

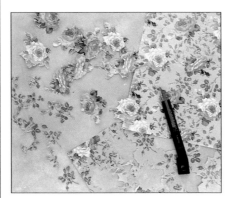

1 Select the paper or prints you would like for your box. I have chosen an old-fashioned rose design that reminds me of a cottage garden, which is ideal for my traditional bedroom scheme. Cut out all the elements you need from the paper.

2 If the box isn't painted, then colour it with at least two coats of emulsion, allowing the coats to dry between each application. Position the cut roses around the lid of the box until you form a design that you are happy with. Stick down with a little PVA glue.

3 Choose a smaller, more detailed print and use as a narrow border around the outside of the box, taking care to glue right up to the edges. Score across the opening of the box with a sharp knife if the flowers overlap this edge. Varnish to protect.

Rosy Tieback

Even the plainest curtains can look really special if you make this simple, yet very pretty, tieback.

MATERIALS

calico fabric

pattern paper

pencil

iron-on interfacing

piping cord

pins

scissors

PVA

household paint brush

spray paint

thread

Hints

I find that any type of spray paint works on the flowers, even car paint, so don't worry about trying to find spray-on fabric paint.

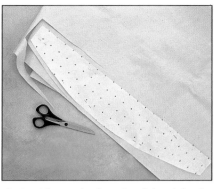

1 Decide on the length of the tieback by measuring around your curtain. Make a template approximately 10cm/4in wide by the length required. Use a pencil to curve the two sides so each measures 4cm/1½in at their ends. Cut two pieces of fabric, adding 1.25cm/½in for turnings.

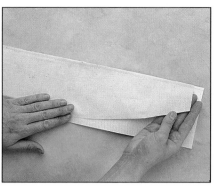

2 Press a piece of heavy weight, iron-on interfacing to one of the tieback shapes. Use only enough pressure on the iron to hold the interfacing in place as this will be trimmed later.

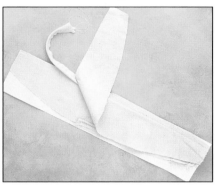

3 Cover enough piping cord to go all the way around the tieback. Raw edges together, pin and stitch this to the stiffened tie-back. Take the second tieback piece, and right sides together, sandwich the piping between, pin then sew along the top edge only.

4 Trim seam allowances on stiffened piece and turn right side out. Cut two pieces of fabric 2.5 x 5cm/1 x 2in. Turn under the raw edges and stitch closed. Fold each in half to form two loops. Place each inside the narrow edges of the tieback and stitch in place.

5 Thin PVA with an equal quantity of water and brush over a piece of calico to stiffen. When dry cut into 15 x 4cm/6 x 1¾in strips. Fold these in half. At one end fold in the two corners to form a triangular shape.

6 Hold the base of six petals to create a rose. Bind the base with strong thread. Cut out a leaf shape from the stiffened calico. Use red spray paint to colour the roses and green for the leaves. Sew or stick roses and leaves to the tieback.

Wastepaper Bin

This is designed as a cover for an ugly plastic waste bin. Simply slot it over your bin for a stylish way to dispose of rubbish.

MATERIALS

tape measure

coloured cardboard

pencil

ruler

stencil

craft knife

hole punch

coloured raffia

scissors

Hints

If you don't have a stencil you could simply draw around an object with an interesting outline.

1 Measure the sides and base of your wastepaper bin. Add 6mm/1/4in all round for an easier fit. Cut four sides and one base panel from the coloured cardboard to these dimensions. Position your stencil on the cardboard. My seahorse is centrally placed 5cm/2in below the top edge. Draw around the stencil outline.

2 Cut out the seahorse using a craft knife. Draw a line 2.5cm/1in in from the edges of the five panels (except for the top edge of each side panel). Mark points at 5cm/2in intervals along this line with a pencil. Use the hole punch to make holes at these points.

3 Cut the coloured raffia into 12.5cm/5in lengths. Position two side pieces side by side and thread the raffia through the top hole in each. Tie in a bow. Repeat for all the other holes. Assemble remaining sides and base panel in the same way until wastepaper bin cover is complete.

CHILDREN'S ROOM PROJECTS

The beauty of making these projects is that you will get as much pleasure out of making them as your children will have using them. Many of the projects are practical yet fun for kids to make, such as the rag doll tiebacks on page 212 which are made from scraps of fabric and can be easily detached and washed if little sticky fingers find them too hard to resist playing with. You can create the colourful sunflower holdbacks on page 220, trim a blind with the seashore edging on page 206 or stencil the flowered floorcloth on page 214, which is particularly lovely for a little girl's room. Both boys and girls will appreciate the chunky dinosaur curtain edging on page 218 and the blanket box on page 210. For a new baby there is a comforting quilt on page 204, and as they grow older the padded number curtains on page 216 will help them learn to count. You can rediscover the delights of folding and cutting paper with your children as you make the lampshade on page 224, and have great fun using fabric paints to create the animal cushions on page 208.

Baby Quilt

This padded quilt is designed to be reversible so the front and back are made in the same way.

MATERIALS

patterned fabric

scissors

needle

thread

pins

wadding

narrow ribbon

Hints

If you want ribbons on both the front and back of the quilt simply turn the quilt over and repeat the procedure making sure the bows are in the same place on each side.

1 Cut two main pieces for the quilt 50cm/20in square and eight border strips 10 x 100cm/4 x 40in. Cut the ends of each strip at an angle of 45 degrees to form a mitre. Hand sew along the top and bottom of each strip to gather.

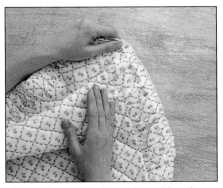

2 Pin then tack the gathered borders to the four sides of each main piece, adjusting the gathers to fit the corners. Machine sew each mitred corner carefully, then machine sew the border in place, ensuring that the gathers are even. Press the gathers flat.

3 Cut two pieces of wadding to the size of the completed front and back pieces. I have shown you the stitching lines on the wadding, but you could sew the wadding to the fabric following the diagonal lines of the patterned fabric. Stop before you reach the border edge.

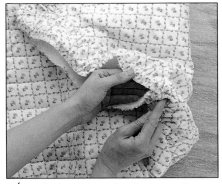

4 With the right sides facing and raw edges even, pin the quilted pieces together. Machine sew the seams, remembering to leave a gap on one side, wide enough to turn the quilt through. When the quilt is pulled through hand stitch the gap closed using a needle and matching thread.

5 Thread the narrow ribbon through a needle and push the needle through all the layers of quilted fabric from front to back then to the front again. Cut the ribbon and tie securely using a double knot then a bow.

Seashore Blind Edging

Capturing the memories of summer holidays, this edging is perfect for a child's room or bathroom.

MATERIALS

pencil

cardboard

scissors

paper pulp

white emulsion

bowl

artist's paint brush

artist's acrylic paints

gloss varnish

needle

strong thread

blind

Hints

You could use a child's drawings as inspiration for these sea creatures or get your children to draw their own shapes on cardboard.

1 Draw elementary fish shapes onto a piece of cardboard. Include a simple starfish and a three pronged outline to resemble seaweed. Cut out the shapes and sandwich between two layers of paper pulp. The finished shape should be at least 1.2cm/1/2in thick.

2 Allow the shapes to dry. Pour a little white emulsion paint into a bowl and paint both sides of the shapes. Apply enough layers of paint to achieve the surface you want. Let each coat dry before applying the next to achieve a smooth finish.

3 Use acrylic paints to colour the fish and seaweed. Refer to children's story books, if necessary, for colour and detail ideas. When dry apply gloss varnish to protect. Use a darning needle to pierce each shape, then sew to the blind hem with strong thread.

Animal Cushions

These brightly painted cushions can also be used as toys. An older child can paint the animals using coloured fabric paint. Remember to seal the paint by ironing.

MATERIALS

pattern paper

pins

calico fabric

scissors

filling

needle

thread

fabric paint

artist's paint brush

Hints

Enlarge your child's animal drawings on a photocopier and use as patterns for the cushions.

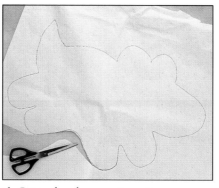

1 Draw the shape onto pattern paper. Your sewing line will be 1.25cm/½in inside this line. Remember the simplest shapes often look best. Pin the paper template onto a piece of double thickness, calico fabric. Cut carefully around the outline.

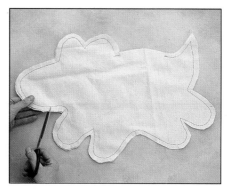

2 Sew all around the shape keeping your seam allowances even. Leave an opening of 10cm/4in for turning the shape through. Snip the curves almost up to the sewing line to ease the corners.

3 Turn the animal shape to the right side and stuff firmly using a suitable filling. Take care when choosing your filling, you will find several safe hygienic fillings on the market that are suitable for small children. Sew the opening together.

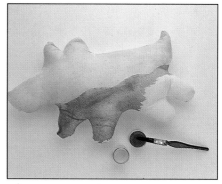

4 Using brightly coloured fabric paints, shade in the animal details onto the calico shape. These can be as realistic or as fanciful as you wish.

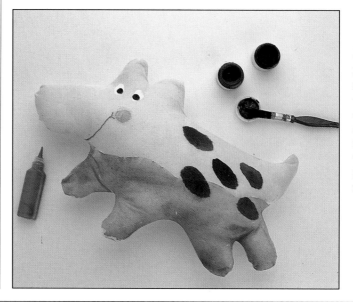

5 Use your imagination and over emphasise all the facial markings for a dramatic look. I used blobs of paint on my fingertips to create the eyes; a tube of fabric paint with a nozzle is ideal for painting the animal's smile.

Blanket Box

You can often find old blanket boxes or ottomans in second-hand shops, so watch out for the bargains.

MATERIALS

fabric	scissors
wadding	staple gun/tacks
pattern paper	tape measure
PVA	

1 Measure lid, sides and plinth of box. Add 1.25cm/½in all around to the sides and plinth for turnings and an extra 4cm/1¾in around the lid. Transfer the dimensions to pattern paper. Cut out the templates and then the fabric pieces.

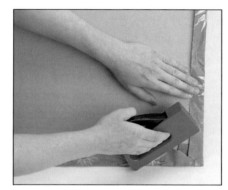

2 Cut a piece of wadding to the exact size of the lid to make a softly padded top. Use a little PVA to glue this in place on the lid. Position the fabric over the wadding on the lid and fit loosely to the inside of the lid with a staple gun or small tacks.

3 Cover the front of the box with PVA glue. Position the fabric, smoothing out from the centre. Turn the excess fabric to the inside of the box and around to the two sides. Glue in place. Repeat for the back. When covering the sides, fold in turnings and glue down for a neat edge. Paint any decorative details in a contrasting colour.

4 Use a staple gun or tacks to firmly secure the fabric to the lid, keeping the fabric tight throughout. At each corner fold the fabric carefully to achieve a mitred finish. Cut a piece of fabric to line the lid. Fold in turnings and glue in place.

Rag Doll Tiebacks

These delightful dolls are joined together with touch-and-close fastener which means they can be removed for play or cleaning at any time.

MATERIALS

tracing paper	trimmings
pencil	beads
paper	buttons
scissors	wool yarn
fabric pieces	needle
felt pieces (pink, brown, red)	thread
fabric glue	touch-and-close fastener

Hints

Use the touch-and-close fastener on the dolls' hands to attach them to the curtains as well as to make the tiebacks. The dolls can also be separated from each other and replaced in different positions.

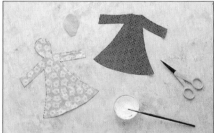

1 Trace the template on this page and enlarge it on a photocopier to an appropriate size. Use the template to cut out a fabric backing for each doll, a dress and pink or brown felt faces. Use different fabrics for each doll. Apply fabric glue over the backing and stick on the dress and face.

2 Decorate the dresses with colourful spots or hearts and flowers all cut from coloured fabric. Use fabric glue to stick them in place. Also stick on whatever decorative trimmings catch your eye: beads or buttons look good, and rickrack braid and pompom edgings look pretty along the hems.

3 Use strands of wool yarn for the hair; a few stitches will hold these in place. Stitch on tiny beads for the eyes and glue on a pair of red felt lips. Make each doll as individual as you can; use yellow, black and red wool yarn for the hair, cutting both long and short strands. Plait strands if you wish.

4 Attach touch-and-close fastener to the dolls' arms to link them together. Two loops of dolls fastened over a hook on either side of each curtain will hold them back. When the curtains are closed the loops may be joined together to form a line of dolls across them.

Stencilled Floorcloth

I love these simple, hard-wearing cloths because you can decorate them in whatever pattern or style you fancy. Let the children decorate their own bedroom cloth, covering the floor with lots of newspaper first. All you need to do is let the paint dry, then protect it with acrylic varnish.

MATERIALS

canvas

scissors

sewing machine

thread

cloth

iron and ironing board

pencil

ruler

emulsion paints

paintbrush

manila paper

craft knife

double-sided tape

stencil brush

Hints

For a completely no-sew project, you can glue the hems down using PVA adhesive.

1 Cut the canvas to the size of cloth you require plus 5cm/2in all around for the hem. Turn the hem under, machine stitch and then press down firmly with a damp cloth and a hot iron. Fold the corners over neatly to avoid any large bumps that will show on the other side.

2 Draw a deep border around all four sides using a pencil and ruler (keep the pencil line as faint as possible). My 122cm/48in cloth has a border of 20cm/8in. Spread lots of newspaper under the cloth prior to painting.

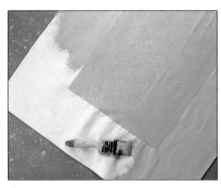

3 Paint in the central area first using two coats of a bright emulsion paint. Brush the paint up to the drawn line but don't despair too much if your line is a little wobbly, it all adds to the character of the cloth. Paint the border using two coats. Allow to dry thoroughly.

4 Enlarge the tulip outline on this page to a suitable size on a photocopier and transfer it on to a piece of manila paper. Cut around the outline carefully using a craft knife. (Thin cardboard will do if you first cut out the design and protect the cardboard with two layers of oil-based paint.)

5 Place small pieces of double-sided tape underneath the stencil and lay the stencil on the border. Stencil tulips using coloured emulsion or acrylic paints, angling one into each corner. Measure the distance between each corner stencil and space more tulips evenly between.

Padded Numbers Curtain

These softly padded numbers can be attached and detached using pieces of touch-and-close fastening stitched at the back of each number and directly onto the curtain fabric. Use your existing curtains or follow the guidelines in the introduction for sewing new ones.

MATERIALS

pencil

paper

ruler

scissors

fabric pieces

pinking scissors (optional)

touch-and-close fastener

needle

thread

chopstick

stuffing

Hints

To make the numbers, draw big numbers on paper and add a border of at least 5cm/2in around each one which will give the numbers a good depth when padded. Cut the templates from the paper and use them to cut out fabric. You will need two fabric pieces for each number.

1 Use your templates (see Hints, opposite) to cut the fabric numbers. To prevent the fabric from fraying, use pinking scissors if you have them. Alternatively, use felt or another non-fraying fabric. Stitch one side of touch-and-close fastener to the back of a number and the other side to the curtains.

2 Sew each number pair together with the wrong sides facing. Keep the stitching line as close to the edge as possible and leave a small gap for stuffing. Pack the stuffing in quite tightly using a chopstick or knitting needle to push the stuffing around the curves. Sew the gap closed and stick the numbers to the curtain.

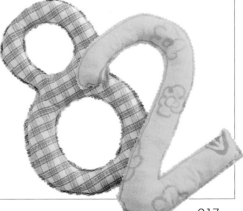

Dinosaur Curtain Edging

Classic gingham checks are used to great effect here to create this clever dinosaur edge for a child's room.

MATERIALS

tracing paper

pencil

paper

scissors

check fabric

gingham fabric

dotted fabric

iron and ironing board

curtain fabric

thread

sewing machine

lining fabric (optional)

Hints

This edging is created from three layers of fabric scallops - you could use fewer or more layers, depending on your time and patience! You will need to place scallops along the width of the curtain, leaving a gap of 5cm/2in between each one.

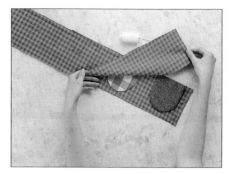

1 Trace the outline on this page and enlarge it on a photocopier to an appropriate size. Use the resulting template to cut out fabric scallop shapes from double thicknesses of fabric. With right sides facing, sew around the curved line of each shape, keeping the stitching as close to the raw edges as possible. Turn the shapes rights sides out and press.

2 Cut two 12.5cm/5in deep borders from the main fabric across its width. Place the first row of scallop shapes along one border piece and sandwich these between the second border piece, with right sides together. Stitch along the top hem leaving a small seam allowance.

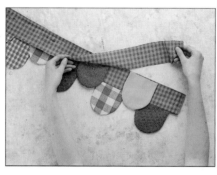

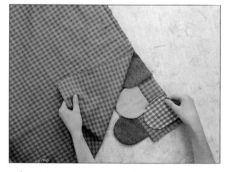

3 Fold the top and bottom border fabrics upwards and press. Fold each border strip inwards, reducing their widths by half and creating a weighted hem to the curtain. Place more scallops along the top edge of this border, positioning them over the gaps formed by the scallops beneath. Then with right sides facing, sew a half-width border (6.25cm/2 1/2in) across them.

4 Place yet another line of scallops along this top edge to produce the third layer of decoration. With right sides together, pin then stitch the bottom edge of the curtain fabric over the border. Keep the fabric taut as you feed the fabric under the sewing foot to avoid unnecessary gathers.

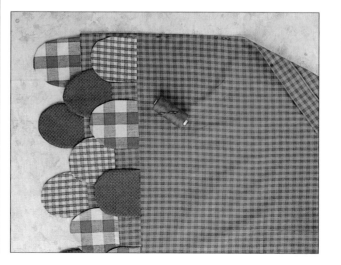

5 Turn under a double hem down the side of the curtain and press. Make up your chosen curtain heading to finish.

Sunflower Holdbacks

These attractive holdbacks look particularly good with lightweight cotton or muslin fabrics.

Hints

Bright-coloured felt is the best material for the sunflower petals; most other fabrics would fray when cut.

1 Using the top half of the self-cover button as a guide and for each holdback, cut a circle from the brown felt to make the centre of the sunflower. Enlarge the petal outline on this page on a photocopier to an appropriate size, and use this as a template to cut out the yellow felt petals. Glue tiny circles of black felt onto the brown felt circle.

2 To add further interest to the centre of the flower, sew tiny black beads between the black felt circles, and also stitch French knots of black wool yarn for extra texture. If you have small children it may be advisable to secure the black felt spots with a stitch or two to prevent them from being pulled off.

3 Cover the self-cover button with the sunflower centre, folding over the excess felt. Place the yellow petals over the back of the button and press the two halves together. Screw the fixings to the base of the holdbacks and attach them to your wall.

Crown Curtain Heading

Tired of looking at conventional curtain headings? This unique, pointed heading certainly adds a flourish to the top of any curtain.

MATERIALS

curtain fabric

backing fabric

paper

pencil

thread

sewing machine

scissors

chalk

needle

pompoms

heading tape

curtain hooks

Hints

This bright fabric would add a splash of colour to a child's room or a nursery, or simply substitute a natural, creamy-coloured fabric for an up-to-the-minute look for a living room or bedroom.

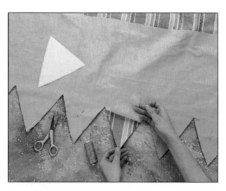

1 Measure your window carefully and follow the guidelines in the introduction for making up a simple unlined curtain. As this curtain is not lined, cut a piece of backing fabric to cover the pointed edge and extend below any tape or gathering lines. To make sure the points remain consistent, cut a paper template and use this to cut out the main and backing fabrics at the same time. Pin together with right sides facing.

2 Stitch around the heading. For a continuous stitching line, stop the machine at the top and bottom of each point, making sure the needle is through all thicknesses of fabric. Then lift the foot, turn the fabric, replace the foot and continue. Clip into the points and turn the heading to the right side.

3 For a decorative flourish you may wish to sew little pompoms on top of each point. These can be bought at craft or department stores, but if you have difficulty obtaining them, you could make your own or choose an alternative, such as beads or buttons.

4 Turn the fabric over to the reverse side and pin then stitch a standard curtain heading tape just below the pointed heading. Stitch over the ends and use the cords to gather up the heading. Tug each point gently and slip curtain hooks into the gathered tape to hang the curtain.

Child's Lampshade

This decoration uses the old-fashioned technique of folding and cutting paper, but I've replaced the traditional doll with this jaunty chicken.

MATERIALS

photocopied chicken

black cartridge paper

pencil

scissors

glue

paper lampshade

needle

thread

Hints

Cut a row of complete chickens - no halves - and position on the lampshade at the most convenient height.

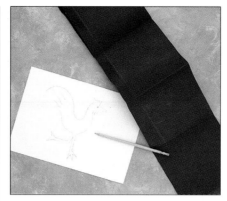

1 Enlarge our chicken shape by 200% on a photocopier to quadruple its size. Cut a strip of black paper to the width of the chicken's height. Draw around the chicken, then concertina fold the paper ensuring that the chicken's leg and beak overlap the folds.

2 Cut around the chicken shape through two or three folds of paper at one time. Use the last cut-out chicken shape as the cutting line for the next three folds. Repeat the process until you have cut out enough chickens to go around the shade.

3 Join the last chicken to the first with a little glue and position this band onto the lampshade. Sew through the top of each chicken head and tail using a loose stitch to secure it in place. Fit the shade in place.

Appliqué Pocket Tiebacks

Not only do these tiebacks look pretty, they are functional as well. Use the little pocket to store potpourri, or to hold small bunches of sweet-smelling lavender.

MATERIALS

various fabrics

scissors

self-cover buttons

needle and thread

beads

tracing paper

pencil

paper

sewing machine

string

fusible interfacing

brass rings

brass hooks

Hints

To make a template for your tiebacks, pass a cloth tape measure around your curtains at the point where the tiebacks will be. Transfer this measurement onto paper, then draw a crescent shape around the line, referring to the shape shown in Step 6.

1   For each tieback, cut a small circle of fabric wide enough to place over the self-cover button and sew tiny beads over the fabric to decorate it. Lay the beaded fabric over the top half of the button and tuck the raw edges to the inside. Place the second half over this and snap the two pieces together.

2   Cut out two pieces of fabric for the pocket back (17 x 20cm/$6^1/2$ x 8in) and a smaller rectangle for the pocket front (17 x 18cm/$6^1/2$ x $6^3/4$in). Fold back the top of the pocket front and stitch in place. Trace the heart motif on this page and enlarge it on a photocopier to an appropriate size. Use this template to cut out a fabric heart and pin it onto the front of the pocket. Hold in place with long running stitches worked by hand.

3   Insert the pocket front between the two pieces of pocket back fabric (their right sides should be facing). Stitch the pocket pieces together along three sides. Turn right sides out and hand stitch the remaining gap closed.

4   Place a small rectangular scrap of fabric over the area at the top of the pocket flap, with right sides facing, and stitch a buttonhole over this. Cut into the buttonhole and push the excess fabric through to the wrong side.

5   Cut out the tiebacks as directed in Hints, opposite. For a stiffer tieback, include a layer of fusible interfacing between the two layers of fabric.

6   Stitch the two fabric pieces together with right sides facing, leaving a small gap to turn to the right side. Turn and then stitch the gap closed with small hand stitches. Sew the button in place and fix on the appliqué pocket. Sew two brass rings to the ends of each tieback.

BATHROOM PROJECTS

Whether painted in relaxing blues and vibrant greens to give a Mediterranean feel, or pastel shades in the faded wash of a beloved old beachhut, your bathroom is a good room to have fun with when it comes to decorating. Experiment with colour-washing techniques (see page 236) and add delicate touches such as the glass-painted storage bottles on page 248. Alternatively, why not try a sea theme in your bathroom?

Sew shells to the bottom of a shower curtain (see page 252) and decorate in azure blues and deep turquoises to bring to mind the ocean and create a wonderful feeling of tranquillity. Frame your window with the crackled shell pelmet on page 244 and personalize your bathroom with favourite beach-combing finds from past holidays.

Create your very own spa in which to completely relax and pamper yourself by frosting your windows as shown on page 250, making the sand-cast candles on page 246 and adding elegant accessories, such as the lapis lazuli candlestick on page 238.

Sink Cabinet

This cabinet has a real beachcomber look, even the handles are made from pieces of driftwood.

MATERIALS

cabinet

white acrylic primer

2 colours of emulsion paint

paintbrush

sandpaper (coarse and medium grades)

Hints

Choose colours that are close in tone for this cabinet and wear the colours away as little or as much as you like - continually assess the distressing process as you work.

1 Paint the cabinet with the white acrylic primer and allow to dry. Make sure all the wood is covered well as the humid conditions in a bathroom are not very kind to wooden furniture.

2 Loosely brush on coats of coloured emulsion paint, layering one coat on top of another but allowing one coat to dry before applying the next. Don't worry about trying to achieve an even layer of colour.

3 Sand the whole cabinet down using first coarse then medium grade sandpaper, controlling the amount of paint removal as you work.

4 Screw a handle in place, or use a piece of driftwood if you prefer.

Seashell Cabinet

This cabinet can be hung on the wall or placed on a surface to be used as a glass-lidded display box for pretty soaps and bathroom accessories.

MATERIALS

bathroom cabinet

sandpaper (medium and fine grades)

thin cardboard

pencil

scissors

masking fluid

fine paintbrush

coloured emulsion paints

paintbrush

acrylic varnish

Hints

Paint starfish or fishes on this box as an alternative to these pink scallop shells.

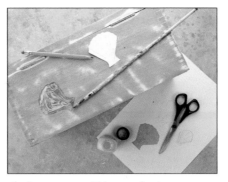

1 Remove any old layers of paint or varnish if you are recycling an old cabinet. Transfer the shell on this page on to thin cardboard and cut along the outline carefully to make a simple stencil. Place the stencil on the cabinet and hold in place. Paint masking fluid between the shell outline and allow to dry.

2 Paint the base colour emulsion over the cabinet; for a more interesting effect, brush the colour on patchily. When the emulsion paint is quite dry, rub the surface of the masking fluid with your finger to start the peeling process, then peel it away to reveal the bare wood. Rub the surface lightly with sandpaper.

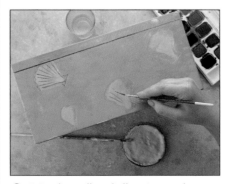

3 Paint the scallop shells using patchy areas of pink colour - don't worry if some of the raw wood shows through. When this is dry, add the fine shell details using a fine paintbrush. Seal and protect the cabinet with two layers of acrylic varnish.

Bathroom Chair

Because this cover is made from soft, absorbent towelling fabric it is ideal for use in a bathroom.

MATERIALS

pattern paper

scissors

pins

towelling

dinner plate

needle

thread

lining fabric

foam padding

bias binding

Hints

Use a long stitch on your sewing machine to stop the towelling from puckering. Zigzag over the edges of each piece before sewing to prevent the towelling from fraying.

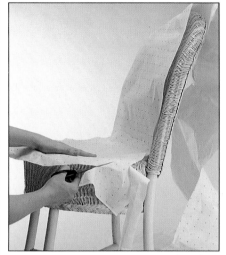

1 Position pattern paper over the chair and cut templates for each of the main pieces. Every chair will be different but generally you will need templates for the seat; from seat to top; from back to the floor and finally a skirt to cover the legs around the sides and front of the chair.

2 Pin each template to one thickness of towelling. Cut around the template adding 1.25cm/½in all round for the seam allowance. Use the chair to pin the pieces together adjusting them to fit. Sew the seams and press open. Position back on the chair to check the fit is correct.

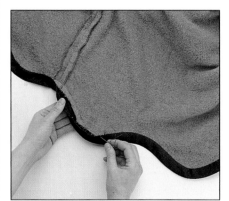

3 Cut a wavy hem all round the bottom edge of the cover. Use a dinner plate to cut the curves accurately, adjusting the measurements to create an even number of curves. Right sides facing, sew bias binding to the hem. Fold over the binding to the back of the cover sandwiching the raw edge in between and hand sew to finish.

4 Using the seat template cut a single piece of lining fabric then cut two pieces of towelling, adding 2.5cm/1in seam allowance. Sew all three pieces together using the lining cloth as a sewing guide. Leave a turning gap. Turn the cover to the right side. Fill with foam, cut to the same size. Sew up the opening.

Colour-washed Tongue and Groove Panelling

Colour washing gives a stunning Mediterranean feel to any room or surface so don't be afraid to use the brightest colours you can find.

MATERIALS

2 oil based paint colours

white spirit

paint kettle

5cm/2in paint brush

knotting sealer

Hints

As an alternative treatment it is possible to create this effect using thinned emulsion paints washed over a prepared emulsion base coat. For the best results choose a base colour that's similar to the glaze. You will need to varnish it when finished.

1 On new panelling it is important to let the natural wood grain show through, so there is no need to prepare with a base coat, but it is essential to seal any knots in the wood with the relevant preparation to prevent any wood resins from seeping through the paint.

2 Dilute the two colours to be used with an equal quantity of white spirit in a paint kettle. Apply the darkest colour directly on to the panelling first. Brush the paint outwards so the colour is stronger in some areas and lighter in others.

3 When the first coat is completely dry apply the second colour in the same way. Leave stronger patches of colour in some areas but work the paint well into other areas for a softer look. Take care to avoid making an obvious pattern.

Lapis Lazuli Candlestick

Lapis lazuli is actually a blue mineral used as a gemstone which is also in the pigment of ultramarine blue. I think this treatment is such a beautiful way to transform a plain candlestick into an elegant centrepiece.

MATERIALS

tubes of artist's oil colours
(French ultramarine and Coeruleum blue)

gold paint

artist's paint brush

Fitch brush (or soft artist's brush)

Softening brush
(or long-haired paint brush)

fine-grade sandpaper

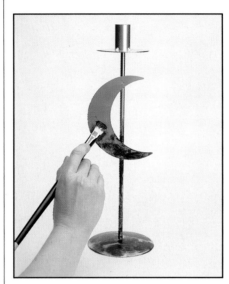

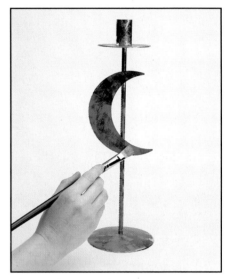

1 'Key' the surface of the metal or wooden candlestick with fine- grade sandpaper. For this treatment there is no need for a base coat. Use the Fitch brush to dab on the ultramarine oil colour in patchy areas.

2 Use the second, Coeruleum blue, oil colour, to fill in the gaps and slightly overlap the first colour. Blend the colours together with a softening brush so that there are no hard edges.

3 Dip the artist's paint brush into the gold paint and apply randomly over the surface of the candlestick to create glinting highlights.

As this candlestick is purely decorative, it is not necessary to coat with any protective varnish.

238

Bath Mat

Stepping out of a bath onto a really soft mat is, I think, the finishing touch to bathtime luxury.

MATERIALS

towelling

thread

needle

scissors

Hints

When you plait towelling, which is quite bulky, you will get a better result if you work quite loosely – your mat will also come together much quicker.

Preparation

Cut the towelling into nine strips approximately 15cm/6in wide by 90cm/36in long. Sew the lengths together so that you will have three long lengths. It is a good idea to shake the cut towelling at this stage to remove any loose threads.

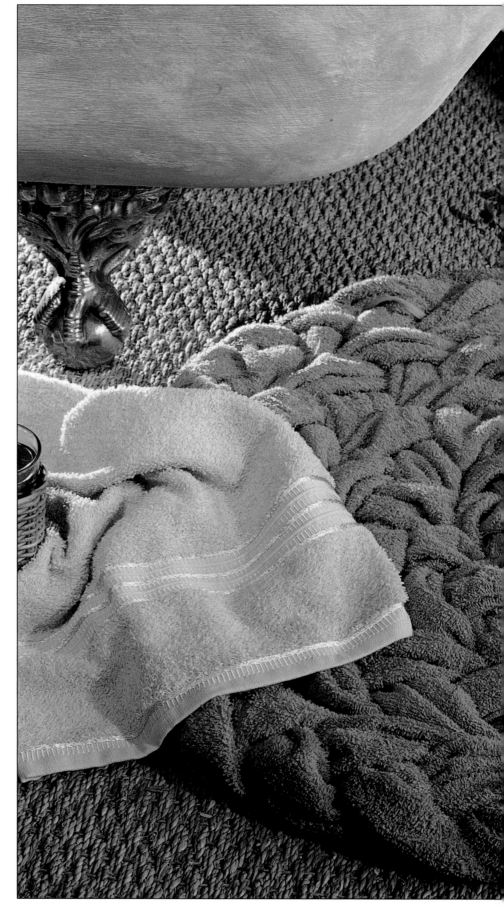

1 To prevent the side edges from fraying oversew using the long zigzag stitch on your sewing machine. This may seem rather time consuming but it is worth it because otherwise you will find that your mat will start to disintegrate the first time it goes into the washing machine.

2 Place the three strips on top of each other and sew together along the top edge. Plait the strips in the usual manner, bunching the towelling and turning the edges underneath as you do so. It may be easier to work on the floor at this stage. Secure final edge.

3 Carefully turn the plait over. Coil one end around into an oval shape. Using a large needle and strong thread, sew the coiled edges together. The stitches can be quite large as you will not be able to see them. Continue coiling until you have finished. Tuck in the end and sew securely.

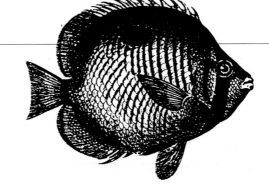

Marine Cabinet

A simple glass-fronted cabinet can be transformed, with a few basic materials and a little imagination, to resemble the look of patterned glass.

MATERIALS

scissors

self-adhesive clear plastic

bathroom cabinet

coloured tissue paper

photocopied fish pictures

PVA glue

watercolours

artist's paint brush

Hints

If you can find only coloured pictures of fish, you can colour- photocopy them, but I think hand-tinted ones look more original.

1 Cut a piece of self-adhesive clear plastic to the same internal measurements as the glass panel in your cabinet door. Place the plastic, clear side facing down, on the front of the door panel, then peel off its backing paper, sticky side is uppermost.

2 Tear strips of coloured tissue paper and place these in vertical, overlapping lines, on the plastic to resemble seaweed. Arrange the "seaweed" strips to look decoratively pleasing with equal spaces between each line.

3 Select your fish pictures and photocopy them, enlarging or reducing their size to fit. Cut out carefully and stick over the tissue panels with PVA glue. Tint each fish with watercolours, allowing the print to show through. Remove the completed panel and stick to the inside of the glass door panel.

Crackled Shell Pelmet

This pelmet would be perfectly suited to a bathroom, or in a child's room where the shells can capture the children's attention.

MATERIALS

plywood or MDF

tape measure

saw

fret saw

emulsion paint (2 colours)

paintbrushes

crackle varnish

shells

sandpaper (coarse-grade)

bonding glue

right-angled brackets

screws

Hints

Cut out a wavy edge from a sheet of plywood, following the instructions outlined for the Fruity Découpage Pelmet on page 138.

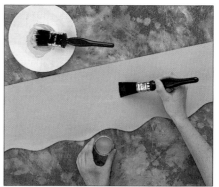

1 Paint the pelmet with two coats of a medium blue emulsion paint. Leave it to dry thoroughly and then apply a thin layer of crackle varnish. Paint the varnish in one direction only.

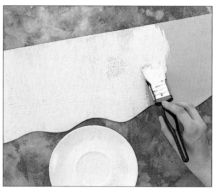

2 Paint a layer of cream emulsion paint over the dry crackle varnish. Load the paintbrush with paint and work quickly; you will see the cracks start forming almost as soon as the emulsion paint goes on. Leave to dry.

3 To make bonding easier, rub the base of each shell with a coarse-grade sandpaper to scratch the surface underneath. Use a strong bonding glue to glue the shells along the edge of the pelmet. Attach the pelmet as described on page 138.

Sand-cast Candles

Colour the melted wax with wax crayons; the more crayons you add, the stronger will be the colour of the candle. A quantity of 450g/1lb of wax will make three or four small candles or one large one.

MATERIALS

plastic bowl or bucket

damp sand

starfish or shells

spray bottle

candle wax

wax crayons

tin can or old pan

large pan

oven mitt

old plastic glove

candle wick

plastic jug

scissors

Hints

If you don't have anything suitable for the mould, simply dig a hole with your hand. For pretty decoration, seashells can then be pressed into the sides of the hole with the shells' right sides facing the sand.

1 Fill the plastic bowl with damp sand and press your starfish or shells into this. Remove the object to reveal the impression in the sand. If you have a poor impression, dampen the sand again and repeat.

2 Spray the impression with water to prevent the sand crumbling. Melt the wax and crayons over the stove in a tin can or an old pan set over another pan of water, continually stirring.

3 Wearing the old plastic glove, dip a piece of wick 10cm/4in longer than your candle into the wax and allow to cool. Still wearing the glove, push the wick into the sand hole and hold it straight while you carefully pour the melted wax from the plastic jug into the mould in a steady stream. Hold the wick straight until the wax cools and it can support itself; then leave the candle to set for a few hours until it is hard. Dig it out of the sand, trim the wick and dust off any loose sand: it is part of the attraction if a little sand sticks to the surface of the wax.

Glass-painted Storage Bottles

These glass bottles look particularly attractive in a bathroom setting and can be used to hold bath oils or lotions.

MATERIALS

specialist glass paint colours

paint tray

wooden skewer

plastic bag

Hints

Two or more glass paint colours can be swirled together in the water to create an interesting pattern.

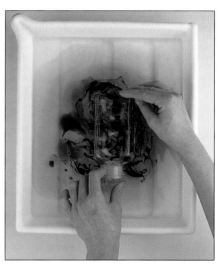

1 Fill a paint tray with water and dribble in a few drops of the glass paint. These will float on the surface so you will need to swirl them around thoroughly with a skewer. The colour does not blend into the water but remains as swirls in the water.

2 Briefly dip the glass bottle into the paint tray to coat one side with the solution. Remove and rotate the bottle before dipping again in the solution to coat the other side. Any paint on your fingers may be easily cleaned with white spirit.

3 Stand on a plastic bag to dry. The colours won't run. Simply peel the bag away from the base of the bottles once they are dry.

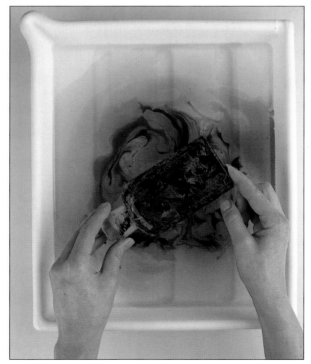

Frosted Glass Effect

Small bathroom windows are perfect for this 'trick' version of frosted glass.

MATERIALS

self-adhesive plastic

scissors

pencil

oil paint

polyurethane varnish

saucer

stencilling brush

Hints

Dab off the excess paint onto a piece of scrap paper so that you are stencilling with only a small amount of paint. Any drips are therefore kept to a minimum - essential on a vertical surface.

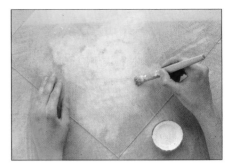

1 Cut out a variety of twists and curls from a sheet of self-adhesive plastic: draw your own or use the outlines on this page as a guide. Peel off the backing paper and place the curls on the glass.

2 Mix together equal quantities of white oil paint and polyurethane varnish; a tablespoon of each should be sufficient for a small window. Use a stencilling brush to apply the paint to the glass, tapping the brush against the surface.

3 Leave the painted surface to dry completely before removing the plastic curls and revealing the design underneath. You may need to lift up the corner of each motif with a craft knife or a pair of scissors.

Shower Curtain

There's no reason for you to live with a boring plastic shower curtain when you can have one as beautiful as this.

MATERIALS

organza

plastic

scissors

tissue paper

thread

eyelet punch

metal eyelets

scallop shells

emulsion paint

brush

soft cloth

drill

needle

Hints

Place tissue paper between the organza and the plastic shower curtain to stop the fabric from slipping and to make the sewing easier.

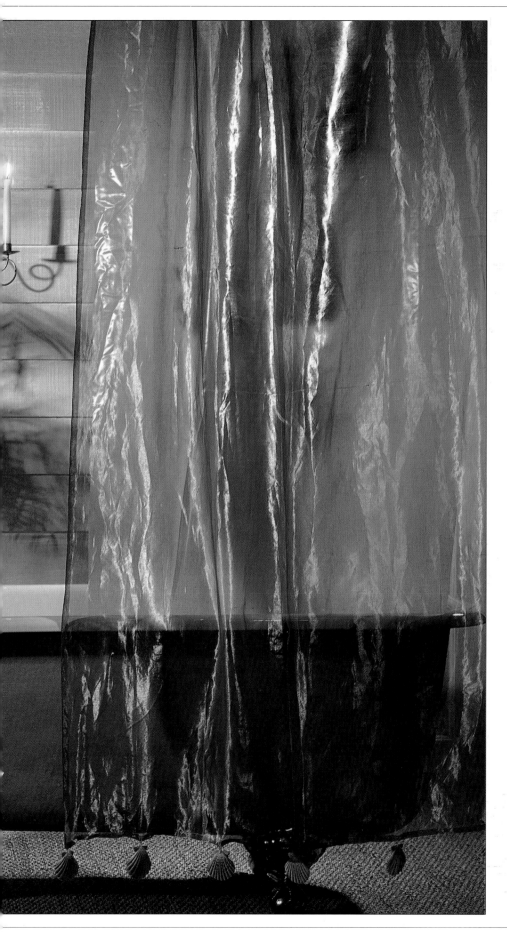

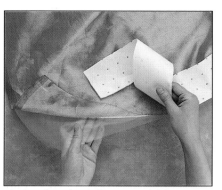

1 Cut the plastic lining and fabric to the required shower curtain length. Allow 2.5cm/1in for seams along the top of the plastic and at top and bottom edges of the organza. Turn in seams and sew organza to the plastic on the top edge. Sew the bottom hem.

2 Use the punch to form the eyelets along the top of the curtain. Space the eyelets at regular intervals making as many eyelet holes as you have hooks. Take care to ensure that the shiny top surface of the eyelet is at the front of the curtain.

3 Use a paint brush to apply a thin layer of very watery emulsion paint to each scallop shell, rub off the excess paint with a soft cotton cloth. Use a drill with a narrow bit to create a tiny hole at the base of each shell. These holes will enable you to sew each shell to the shower curtain hem.

INDEX

ACKNOWLEDGEMENTS

The publishers would like to thank the following companies for providing the merchandise used in our photographs:

A. B. Woodworking, After Noah, Anchor Threads, Artisan, Coats Patons Crafts, Colefax and Fowler, Crucial Trading Co, The Dormy House, Dulux ICI Paints, Dylon International, Anna French, Fun Stamps Ltd, General Trading Company, Global Village, Gore Booker, Graham & Green, Hallmark Cards, C. P. Hart, Hesse and Company, Laura Ashley, Mildred Pearce, The Museum Store, Nice Irma's, Osborne and Little, The Pier, Purves and Purves, Rufflette, Sandersons, Somerset Creative Products, Swish, Tintawn Carpets Ltd, V V Rouleaux.